I'VE KEPT A journal over the past years, and here are some of the comments from folks I've sailed with aboard *Angelique*. — Debbie Seip

"Debbie, what an exceptional series of menus you've provided! I'll particularly remember the delicate seasoning of your great tomato soup. Best of luck!"

LESLIE VEIRS
COLORADO SPRINGS, COLORADO

"You were the icing on the cake of this weekend, Debbie — even more so than the snow!"

LYNNE WALKER
GREENFIELD, MASSACHUSETTS

"Dear Debbie—Thanks for the wonderful introduction to Maine. I never realized the galley was so important to enjoying a vessel. Thanks for the continuous good cheer."

DICK LYON
ANCHORAGE, ALASKA

"Deb, I said it once and I'll say it again and again — this is the BEST food I have ever had — anywhere!! I will always remember this trip because of the food! I'll be back next year, also. Thanks again!!"

SUE BERNSTEIN
STOUGHTON, MASSACHUSETTS

"It's not just your food, Deb. It's you! Your warmth is as warm as the scrumptious breads that come out of that primitive oven. I've always been a meat and potatoes guy, but fish has now entered my scope.

Brownies . . . ? You can always remember me scouting them out! Thanks so much on behalf of all."

MARK BENDER
REGO PARK, NEW YORK

"Debbie, we knew we would eat on this trip, but we had no idea how well we would eat! Mark will be talking about the fish casserole and congo bars for years. I don't know how you do it. 'Happy Sails' to you . . . "

PEGGY VOGTS & MARK MILLER

The Angelique Cookbook
Great Recipes from a
Windjammer's Galley

Gloria,
Have fun
trying my
Recipes at
home.
FairWinds
Captain Debbie Seip

By Debbie Seip

The Yankee Packet Company

PUBLISHED BY THE YANKEE PACKET COMPANY
P O Box 736, Camden, Maine 04843-0736
www.midcoast.com/~sailypc

Library of Congress Cataloging-in-Publication Data

Seip, Debbie
The Angelique cookbook: windjammer home cooking/Debbie Seip
p. cm.
ISBN 0-9656525-0-5
1997

Printed by Regent Publishing Services
June 1997 First Edition
1 3 5 7 9 10 8 6 4 2

Printed In Hong Kong

DEDICATION

In memory of my grandmother, Anna Eckle, "Grammy" to those who knew her and loved her. For her patience and time that she spent having us (my sisters and me) help her cook all those years. I never realized I was learning how to cook.

Marge Wakefield introduced me to Maine Windjammers, and gave me my first *Windjammer World* cookbook. Every time we drove to Deer Isle from Pennsylvania we always stopped in Camden to look at the windjammers. She also encouraged me to try new things and to do more cooking. She has taught me a lot about cooking and has been supplying me with cookbooks and recipe ideas over the years. She is a very special friend and woman!

Barbara (Beam) Margerum is the brave soul who came windjamming with me for the first time, in 1982, on the ketch *Angelique*. We had the best time. She was my moral support when I came up to Camden in 1985 to start working on the *Mercantile*. Then in 1987 she left Pennsylvania with me at 10 PM in a snow storm so that I could meet with Captain Mike and Lynne McHenry the next day. And you all know what I've been doing since!

Mom and Dad for all their support over the years. I can't imagine what they thought when their eldest daughter told them she wanted to cook on a windjammer for the summer and has made it her career. I couldn't have done it without them.

I also need to thank all my loyal passengers for being so persistent over the years about wanting a cookbook.

Contents

FOREWORD

I must down to the seas again, for the call of the
*   running tide*
Is a wild call and a clear call that may not be
*   denied.*

— John Masefield
Sea Fever

A week's sail on *Angelique* in Penobscot Bay reflects in many ways the total Maine experience. It is a pleasurable experience, filled with "good food, plenty of it," warm friends, lots of sun, and a good breeze most of the time. Life on board is relaxed, informal, and comfortable. Everyone enjoys the summer sun, although if you don't like the weather, "just wait a minute," as the saying goes. Maine's weather can change quickly. At times it includes a little fog or some rain, but these only remind us to appreciate good weather when it returns! Truly, anyone who has never witnessed Maine in a fog or a storm has missed a bit of her mystique.

Each windjammer in midcoast Maine has its own individual personality. *Angelique*, in particular, is reminiscent of a grand Maine sea captain's home— it is safe, it is magnificent, it is filled with the romance of the sea, and it is comfortable. Like any good home, *Angelique* has a "room" where company gathers—just off the galley, of course—which has often been the scene of interesting discussion, laughter, music, and even knitting and knot-tying lessons. Angelique's deck offers one of the best views in the world, and it has plenty of room for sprawling comfortably with a book. As you relax, you are often aware of delicious aromas of such delights as fresh bread, yummy brownies, fresh fish chowder, spicy chili, and roast chicken wafting from the galley. Your stomach growls in anticipation. By the week's end, the dinner bell brings out a Pavlovian response.

Many of you who have been passengers on *Angelique* have gone away with a recipe or two, begged from Debbie. Veteran passengers also have gathered a few recipes from the annual *Angelique* newsletter over the years as well. Almost all of you, however, have asked for this cookbook. This book will tell you ingredients and procedures for creating some of those great tastes and smells; you are on your own in creating the proper atmosphere! Memories and imagination will help you out. It may be that some of *Angelique's* foods will be forever linked in your mind with a particular harbor or situation. Blueberry pancakes, perhaps, will always bring back Camden Harbor. For others, spinach salad is reminiscent of a strong wind and lunch on deck, a tricky proposition that may make eating spinach salad a delicious game!

Many of *Angelique's* "food activities" provide entertainment. Perhaps you made new friends while peeling vegetables over a bowl on the deck. Isn't it funny how the allure of peeling and chopping vegetables fades at home? On board, it actually seems fun! Just a bit of proof that magic is afoot. Another magical entertainment is the ice cream-making process. Combine some simple dairy ingredients, ice, salt, and elbow grease, and poof! Ice cream, and it is some delicious! Finally, what is more entertaining than eating lots of lobster on an uninhabited island, letting butter and lobster juices fall where they may? Peeling vegetables, cranking ice cream, smashing lobsters: here are bonding opportunities galore. Some of these events can be recreated only on *Angelique,* so you have to come on board! Other good times, like sharing chili, chowder, or Congo bars over a board game, a card game, or a discussion, you can try to recreate at home. As everyone knows, good food is the most basic ingredient of any enjoyable experience. Always, in the background of a sail on *Angelique,* is the presence of Debbie's cooking.

Food preparation on board any sailing vessel is a result of meticulous planning and Yankee ingeniuty. It is a heroic venture every week. Perils abound which would send most cooks packing: great sailing does not make for great cooking conditions. Sometimes things simply don't stand still. Sometimes Captain McHenry tacks at a time that is not opportune for the biscuits. There is no corner store from which to quickly grab missing ingredients; there is no roomy refrigerator; and the galley itself is, to put it mildly, small. Yet *Angelique's* Debbie the Great, seemingly without effort, produces all manner of goodies from within that small space. She uses Maine ingredients and makes purchases from local suppliers as often as possible. She throws together pie crusts, cookies, bread, biscuits, and sauces in a stress-free, off the cuff manner. No "store bought" goods will be found here! She chats amiably with passengers, jokes with the crew, and comments on the scenery and other boats as we pass them, all the while creating great meals from scratch. This produces the impression that she has special powers. Magic, you know. Uncanny.

Somehow this feeling of magic is not out of place on Penobscot Bay. It is one of the most beautiful and relaxing places on earth. The blues and greens of the sky and water blend around the irregular shapes of the many islands. These island ingredients of sand, granite, and fir trees combine to offer interesting contrast to the eye. Some islands are inhabited by humans, some by birds and seals. One rarely sees the humans, and often only their homes and machines show they exist at all. The seals and birds are much more curious; they stare back. You would think that these creatures would have tired by now of seeing people on ships: since the seventeenth century, Penobscot Bay has been crossed by many vessels, primarily fishing vessels, cargo vessels, and yachts. The designs of the boats change, but their purposes remain the same.

As *Angelique* crisscrosses the bay, passengers see the local fishermen hauling traps, cargo ships headed for Searsport or Rockland, and the beautiful yachts which come from all over the world each year to enjoy the beauty and spectacular sailing that Maine's Penobscot Bay offers. Every windjamming passenger acquires an affinity for special places on the bay. Perhaps your favorite spot is the comfort of Pulpit Harbor, with its osprey nest high on a rock at its "hidden" harbor entrance. Perhaps it is the bustle and beauty of the Fox Islands Thoroughfare, where the Great Schooner Race begins each year. Maybe you long to walk the streets of North Haven and visit the yarn shop there, or sail lazily along the coast of Islesboro, viewing its beautiful homes. The mournful notes of Mark Island Light may fill your memory, or perhaps the stalwart settlement of Stonington calls you back. Do sailing under the bridge at Eggemoggin Reach, or marveling at Somes Sound, the only fjord on the eastern seaboard, or indulging in lobster on the beach of Butter Island comprise your favorite memories? These are the experiences of windjamming on the coast of Maine.

Every now and then there comes a windjammer that is different. *Angelique* is such a vessel. First of all, *Angelique* is not a schooner; she is a ketch. This makes her unique among the Maine windjammers. Like anything in Maine, *Angelique* offers a different aspect depending on your point of view. In design, *Angelique* resembles a rugged Brixham trawler, a hard-working fishing boat that can trace its ship-building tradition as far back as classical times. These original trawlers, which became popular along the British coast in the last century, were smaller than *Angelique;* but the long keel, wide deck and rounded stern are the same. From this hardy design, *Angelique* is stable, solid, and safe. However, *Angelique* has another side: she is also a work of art. She was designed by a Camden resident, Italian-born artist Imero Gobbato. His love for the design of the British working vessel and his intrinsic sense of beauty and clarity of line combined to produce the loveliness of *Angelique*. Physically, then, she is both hard-working and gorgeous.

In purpose *Angelique* is unique as well. Many of the other windjammers in Maine were once working vessels. These historic ships have wooden hulls and were adapted to suit the windjamming passenger trade. Built in 1981, *Angelique* was the first vessel created primarily for the windjamming trade in Maine. As a result, *Angelique* has led the way in providing services and conveniences for her passengers. Her steel hull is appreciated not only by the Coast Guard but also by passengers concerned with safety. Her cabins each offer standing headroom, a fresh-water sink, carpeting, and reading lights in each bunk. Two hot, fresh-water showers below deck lure many to choose *Angelique*. Above, the deck house salon is a great resource in times of rain or chill, and its proximity to the galley keeps it warm for those spring and fall sails. Moreover, it has a piano to gather around in harbor, where folks can sing good old songs together beneath the glow of an oil lamp. Many competitors in the fleet have been quick to try to imitate the *Angelique* experience, but that recipe will never be successfully copied. Its secret lies in the spirit of *Angelique* herself.

Angelique's disciples do offer a suggestion for creating the best vacation in the world: Melt the romance of sailing in a large bay. Throw in several beautiful sunsets, a full moon, and more bright stars than you've ever seen before. Mix well with laughter and discussion. Blend in the sounds of wind in the sails, water lapping at the bow, and a distant lobster boat's engine. Pour into *Angelique* and bake in the sun for three or four months. Store at home in memory and in photo albums, and share readily with friends and family.

Enjoy this collection of recipes from the *Angelique* galley. Experience the magic once more.

Beth Collins
1997

INTRODUCTION

The *Angelique's* galley is different from most windjammers because it is on deck and I have a kerosene-fired stove. I've always said, "I have the best galley in the fleet." The galley is located in the forward section of the deck house, so I have a front-row seat for everything that's going on. There are four windows, two forward and two on either side, and two doors into the deck house; and we get a nice cross-breeze that helps keep the galley and the galley crew at a more normal temperature. This makes cooking aboard a little like cooking at home with the windows wide open and your house tilted and going down the street at eight knots.

I have a Beaufort model Dickinson stove, made in Canada specifically for far-north and marine use. The cooking surface is about 35 x 25 inches. The oven interior is 20 x 20 x 14 inches and has no automatic timer to set. There are no burners as on a conventional range, and the whole top gets hot to various degrees. The left side, being over the fire box, is the hotter side, and adjusting the temperature under pots means moving the pots around till they are cooking the way you want them to. The right side has an 18 x 16 inch griddle area with a groove around it. There is a metal rail that runs around the top of the stove and long fiddles that slip into place to hold the pots and pans steady when *Angelique* is heeling. We have two smoke stacks, or "Charlie Nobles," because we get so much of a down-draft off the mainsail that we have to keep the weather, or windward, stack shut down. The galley area itself is not very big, about 5 x 17 feet, but that keeps me under control!

I've never given the stove a name, although I have to admit to talking to her on occasion in hopes that she will do better. She is, you see, very temperamental, extremely moody, and has a mind of her own. The other thing is that she likes to start her day off slow and easy. So I get up very early to light her up. That's okay because it gives me time to start my prep for the day. It is also the most beautiful part of the day, I think.

A typical day starts at 4 AM when I go topside, light the stove, and get things ready for breakfast. The stove takes another hour to get to cooking temperature so I put the water on and go back to bed below for almost an hour. The rest of my galley crew gets up at 6 AM, and then the fun really begins! We start to make coffee and set up the tables in the mess room for breakfast first. Coffee goes out onto the day-tank at 7 AM. We ring the bell at 8 AM for breakfast below in the mess room. Passengers help bring down the platters of food. (Many passengers suggest that we need a dumbwaiter. Our usual reply is that we have several.) We try to have lunch on deck at noon so that no one misses the scenery. Dinner is around 6 PM in the mess room. Captain Mike tries to have us at anchor for dinner. Then dessert on deck so folks can enjoy the sunset.

We try to get as much prep-work as possible done in the morning so that we can have time to help on deck or just relax in the afternoon. It is an all-day process though—once one meal is done it's on to the next. Although peoples' eating habits have changed since my first season aboard, it's amazing what fresh salt air and a stiff sea breeze can do for your appetite!

I guess I've developed a reputation for being a good cook. When we have new passengers on board it never fails, when I come on board Sunday night, I'm greeted by people saying they've heard from previous passengers all about all the good food we'll be having. No wonder I can't sleep on Sunday nights!

Mondays are very hectic. Most of my time is spent checking and packing the two galley ice boxes. The ice boxes are a big puzzle, because you have to

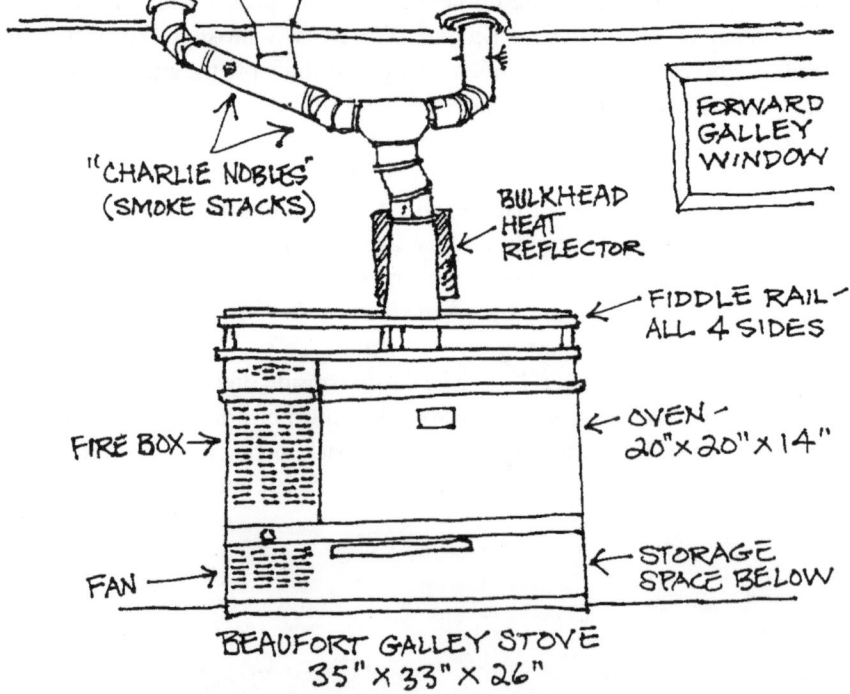

"CHARLIE NOBLES" (SMOKE STACKS)

FORWARD GALLEY WINDOW

BULKHEAD HEAT REFLECTOR

FIDDLE RAIL - ALL 4 SIDES

FIRE BOX →

← OVEN - 20" × 20" × 14"

FAN →

← STORAGE SPACE BELOW

BEAUFORT GALLEY STOVE
35" × 33" × 26"

pack backwards, "Saturday, Friday, Thursday, etc." There is *nothing* worse than digging to the bottom of a packed ice box because something is in the wrong place. My mess cook is busy packing the fruit, vegetables, and other food we have received in the mess room below. No space goes unused. I feel we are very lucky because *Angelique* has a fair amount of storage space. The assistant cook is making blueberry pancakes for breakfast and keeping the coffee pots on deck going and full. Once we leave Camden Harbor we can't be sure we'll be able to restock; so if we've forgotten something, run out of something, or something goes bad, I will sometimes have to improvise.

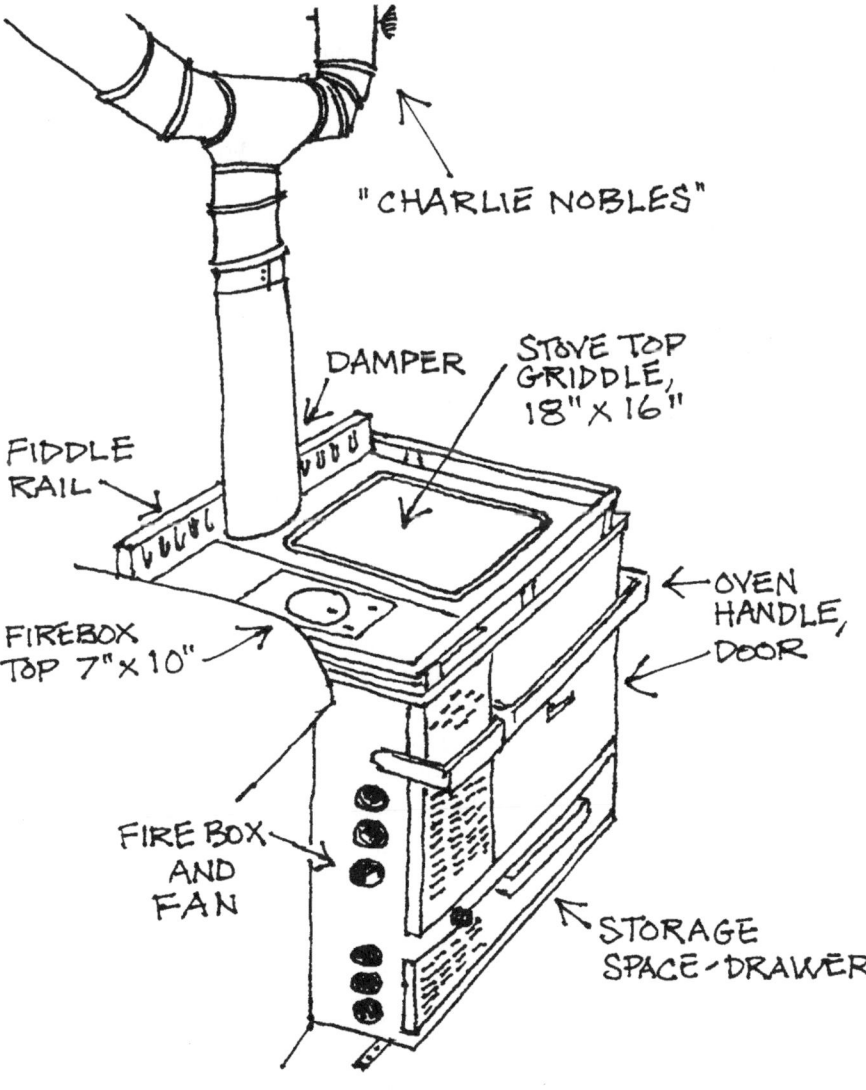

Passengers are always amazed at the way we use every available space on board (hiding places, some people have called them). Unfortunately we will at some time have to ask folks to move so we can get something out of a deck house bench or the starboard side ice box. By midweek I'll only have to walk toward the ice box and people will hop off the lid.

Cooking on a windjammer is very challenging. You never know what the day on board will bring. The weather and wind can really play havoc with food preparation and serving. I always tell my galley crew that the only thing I can promise them is that nothing will be the same twice!!! I give each of my new galley crew a copy of *Windjammer World Cookbook,* by Dee Carstarphen. She does a great job of depicting life on a Maine windjammer, especially life as a "galley slave."

Meals aboard *Angelique* are served family style and include roasts, shipboard-baked pastry, salads and Maine's own seafood. Fresh fruit and vegetables, Maine grown, are delivered to the *Angelique* before she sets sail for a cruise. Lobsters for the island, on-shore bake are bought from wholesalers in various ports — Stonington, Bass Harbor, and Swan's Island, for instance. Special diets are easily accommodated when notice is given.

The menu itself has evolved through years of sailing and cooking aboard with a kerosene-fired marine stove. Appetites flourish in sea air and three hearty meals a day must be planned to be healthy and attractive. There's no overlapping of meals, although, just like home, "leftovers" might show up in a meal later in the week. I like to vary the taste of each dish, and use many different spices to do this. As you will see in the following recipes, I have some favorites, like tarragon in Beef Stew, and tamari, ginger, and cumin in Veggie Stew. Which spices to use and the quantity has come from experience, passengers, and other windjammer cooks. I rely on how a dish appears and tastes to dictate the amount of spice needed. I use mostly dry spices but when possible I use fresh. There is nothing better than fresh rosemary on the Roasted Herb Chicken or fresh parsley and dill in the Chicken Salad. For a full boat of 40 passengers, using dry spices, I start by adding a tablespoon of spice, for a smaller group I start with a teaspoon. You also have to remember that a teaspoon of a hot spice like cayenne pepper or hot paprika can go a long way. When multiplying recipes you do not always want to double or triple the amount of spice.

Cooking aboard the *Angelique* is a partnership with the Beaufort stove. Stove top and oven temperatures are affected by changes in humidity, "breeziness," and deck angle. For example, while under way on cool rainy days things will take longer to cook because the stove does not cook as hot, but on bright breezy days things cook faster because the stover is hotter due to the great drafting effect. And I have often had to wait to put a cake in the oven because *Angelique* was heeling so much the cake would run out of the pan. Hence "tacked cake," where one side is very tall and the other thin as a cookie. Worse yet, it has "valleys and hills" because we tacked several times while it was cooking!

When I started cooking on the *Angelique* I had to spend a lot of time planning the proper cooking order of each meal, because of the limited amount of stove top and oven space. Not only does everything have to be prepared and cooked, but you want it all to be ready for serving at the same time — hot and not over- or under-cooked. This is a major concern because of the quantity of food and size of the pots and pans needed to cook for 40 people. Because there are no automatic timers to set I rely on the way food looks or feels when deciding that it is "finished" cooking rather than time. I have, however, converted on-board cooking times to land-based, home stove times for the recipes in these pages. Breads, though, are done when if you knock on a loaf it sounds hollow!

There are some days when you're afraid to let go of *anything* because you're afraid it will end up on the sole (for landlubbers, the floor) and others when we're heeling so much you have to bend one leg just to keep your balance. I call this the "short-leg syndrome." As a cook you have to wear many hats: cook, mother, counselor, doctor, magician, deck hand, plumber, mind reader, and more. Yes, the list goes on! And I suppose I have as many moods as the Beaufort stove. I do feel that you need to smile a lot, talk to everyone, and, most of all, laugh.

We once sailed in an October snow storm and had to drop anchor in Fox Islands Thoroughfare, North Haven, to have lunch. The pot of chowder was secure on the stove, but the chowder kept lapping out of the pot. One breakfast we served out the galley window with the help of four people, because you couldn't set anything down. But there is always the other side, a beautiful sunny morning in Pretty Marsh or Somes Sound where you have breakfast on deck because no one wants to eat below. Osprey and eagles are over-head and a loon calls in the distance; or you have this great breeze and you're sailing along as the sun is setting. Who would want to have dinner below?

I've learned cooking over the years by cooking. I'm sure I learned a lot from my grandmother; and Marge also helped with all her ideas, recipes, and inspiration.

Many a night was spent at the dinner table with Captain Ted Schmidt talking about his experiences as a windjammer cook and captain. He had many helpful ideas and suggestions, and there was always support and help from other windjammer cooks as well.

It is hard to put into words why I love cooking on a windjammer. One reason is the wonderful people I meet each summer from all over the world with so many life experiences to share; another is the peace and magic of the many islands and bays, and the coast of Maine itself; then there is that joy when you come on board to familiar faces and hugs from folks you've sailed with before, who are back because they understand the magic of windjam-ming along the coast of Maine.

6-DAY MENU

MONDAY

Breakfast

Orange Juice
Cold Cereal
Blueberry Pancakes   17
Sausage

Lunch

Fish Chowder   24
Biscuits   85
Cheese
Carrots & Celery Sticks
Green Olives & Sweet Pickles
Oyster Crackers
Chocolate Brownies   100

Dinner

Roasted Turkey Breast   49
Stuffing   49
Green Bean Casserole   62
Candied Sweet Potatoes   61
Cranberry Sauce   49
Strawberry Shortcake   110

TUESDAY

Breakfast

Cantelope
Granola   15
Scrambled Eggs with Bacon   13
Bran Muffins   86

Lunch

Chicken Salad Sandwiches   21
Corn Chowder   23
or Onion Soup   26
Cucumber Salad   56
Dill Pickles

Dinner

Baked Ham   37
Bean Pot Baked Beans   59
Boston Brown Bread   76
Cole Slaw   55
Apple Crisp   93

WEDNESDAY

Breakfast

Grapefruit Halves	
Hot Cereal	16
Sticky Buns	71

Lunch

Chili with Toppings	22
Corn Bread	77
Corn Chips	
Spinach Salad	57
Raspberry Coconut Squares	109

Dinner

New England Boiled Dinner	45
Mustard Sauce	46
Horse Radish Sauce	
Irish Soda Bread	81
Chocolate Cake	102

THURSDAY

Breakfast

Orange Quarters	
Cold Cereal	
Banana Nut Pancakes	17
Sausage	

Lunch

Creamy Tomato Soup	28
Ham & Cheese Sandwiches	
Anadama Bread	69
Carrot Salad	54
Fresh Fruit Salad	25
(Watermelon Sculpture)	

Dinner

Lobster Bake	42

FRIDAY		SATURDAY

Breakfast

Pineapple Juice	
Granola	15
French Toast with Bacon	14

Lunch

Veggie Stew	30
Tri-Color Bread	83
Waldorf Salad	58
Congo Bars	101

Dinner

Lasagna	40
Garlic Bread	79
Tossed Salad	
Handmade Ice Cream	104

Breakfast/Lunch

On this last day out I sometimes make banana bread or muffins to serve folks with coffee at 7 AM.

Cranberry Juice	
Cold Cereal	
Baked Eggs	13
Fresh Fruit Platters	
Cottage Cheese	

Baked Eggs

Scrambled Eggs

French Toast

Granola

Hot Cereal

Blueberry Pancakes

Banana Walnut Pancakes

Breakfasts

BAKED EGGS

IN GREASED LARGE 13″ x 18″ pan, place approximately 20 slices of bread cut into cubes. I especially like rye or my tri-colored bread, but any bread is fine. I use two large pans, or double this recipe, for a full boat, which is 40 people.

Sprinkle grated cheddar and Swiss cheese on top of bread. Then sprinkle with your choice of leftovers: ham, sausage, bacon, tomatoes, mushrooms, spinach or lobster. Then sprinkle a small amount of cheese on top.

In large mixing bowl beat 12 eggs and 6 cups milk. Pour over bread and cheese.

Bake in a medium oven (350°) for 1$^1/_2$–2 hours or until set.

SCRAMBLED EGGS

I NORMALLY FIGURE 1$^1/_2$–2 eggs per person for scrambled eggs. I double boil the eggs in my stainless steel bowls. Make sure that you spray the bowls well with Pam or some other spray shortening. Keep an eye on the eggs — you have to keep mixing them with a spoon. The only problem is that if you over-cook them, they turn green!

FRENCH TOAST

	10 PEOPLE	20 PEOPLE	40 PEOPLE
eggs	6	12	24
sour cream or yogurt	1/4 pint	1/2 pint	1 pint
vanilla	2 teaspoons	1 tablespoon + 1 teaspoon	3 tablespoons
brown sugar	2 teaspoons	1 tablespoon + 1 teaspoon	3 tablespoons
milk	3 cups	6 cups	12 cups
cinnamon	1–2 tablespoons	3–4 tablespoons	6–8 tablespoons
nutmeg	1/2 teaspoon	1 teaspoon	1 tablespoon
oatmeal bread	1–1 1/2 loaves	2–3 loaves	5–6 loaves

(Some like to use French bread, sliced on the diagonal.)

Combine all ingredients except bread and mix well. Dunk bread slices in this mixture, coating both sides of the bread. Place bread on hot, oiled griddle and brown till golden on both sides.

Sprinkle with powdered sugar and serve with maple syrup on the side.

GRANOLA

	10 PEOPLE	20 PEOPLE	40 PEOPLE
oatmeal	3 cups	6 cups	12 cups
wheat flakes	3/4 cup	1 1/2 cups	3 cups
rye flakes	1/2 cup	1 cup	2 cups
corn meal	2 tablespoons	1/4 cup	1/2 cup
graham cracker crumbs	1/2 cup	1 cup	2 cups
wheat germ	1/2 cup	1 cup	2 cups
sesame seeds	1/4 cup	1/2 cup	1 cup
sunflower seeds	1/4 cup	1/2 cup	1 cup
pumpkin seeds	2 tablespoons	1/4 cup	1/2 cup
walnuts, shelled	3/4 cup	1 1/2 cups	3 cups
pecans	1/2 cup	1 cup	2 cups
almonds	3/4 cup	1 1/2 cups	3 cups
raisins	1 cup	2 cups	4 cups

Mix the above ingredients, *except raisins,* together in a large bowl.

Melt:

	10 PEOPLE	20 PEOPLE	40 PEOPLE
peanut butter in	1/2 pound	1 pound	2 pounds
vegetable oil	2 1/4 teaspoons	1 tablespoon + 1 1/2 teaspoons	3 tablespoons

Add:

	10 PEOPLE	20 PEOPLE	40 PEOPLE
brown sugar	1/4 cup	1/2 cup	1 cup
maple syrup	1/4 cup	1/2 cup	1 cup
honey	1/4 cup	1/2 cup	1 cup
vanilla	1 teaspoon	2 teaspoons	1 tablespoon
cinnamon	1 1/2 teaspoons	1 tablespoon	2 tablespoons

Whisk until mixed well. Pour sauce over dry ingredients gradually. Stir into dry mix, adding a little at a time. Spread onto large cookie sheets.

Bake in a 325°–350° oven until slightly brown, stirring occasionally.

Add raisins after granola has cooled.

HOT CEREAL

FULL BOAT, 40 PEOPLE

oatmeal	³/₄ box
Wheatina	¹/₂ box
wheat germ	¹/₂ jar
brown sugar	to taste
maple syrup	to taste
butter	1 stick
milk	¹/₂–1 cup (more if you like)

Bring 1¹/₂ gallons of water to boil. Add oatmeal, wheat germ and Wheatina. Let cook until done. Then add brown sugar, maple syrup, butter and milk.

If you are making hot cereal for a smaller group of people, just follow the directions on the box.

Breakfast Pancakes

I USE A STANDARD pancake mix, or Bisquick, on board as a time saver. For a full boat, 40 people, I use one 5-pound box. If you are making pancakes for a smaller group of people, follow the directions on the box. Most of the mixes I have call for water, but for best results when using Bisquick, use egg and milk or buttermilk as the instructions on the box indicate.

BLUEBERRY PANCAKES

When making blueberry pancakes for a full boat I use 2 quarts of fresh blueberries or 3–4 bags of frozen blueberries. Rinse frozen berries well before adding to the mix or your pancakes will turn blue-green!

BANANA WALNUT PANCAKES

To make banana walnut pancakes for a full boat, 40 people, I use:

bananas, very ripe, mashed	10
butter	1/4 cup
vanilla	1 tablespoon
walnuts, chopped fine	2 cups

Mash the bananas and add half of the water and vanilla, then slowly stir in the dry mix. Add the remaining water slowly, because you will not need all of it.

On *Angelique's* stove the griddle is hot enough as soon as a few drops of water splashed on it will sizzle. Ladle batter onto the griddle, each pancake about 3"–4" in diameter, about 1/4 cup of batter. I cook 6 at a time. Pancakes are ready to flip when they bubble in the center—first ladled, first flipped.

It takes an hour to cook pancakes for a full boat.

Chicken Salad

Chili

Corn Chowder

Fish Chowder

Fresh Fruit Salad

Onion Soup

Quiche du Jour

Tomato Soup

Veggie Chili

Veggie Stew

Lunches

CHICKEN SALAD

	10 PEOPLE	20 PEOPLE	40 PEOPLE
chicken (fryers), cooked, boned & cut	1–2	3	6
celery, chopped	1¹/₂ cups	3 cups	6 cups
onions, chopped	2 tablespoons	¹/₄ cup	¹/₂ cup
mayonnaise or salad dressing	³/₄ cup	1¹/₂ cups	3 cups
lemon juice	1¹/₂ teaspoons	1 tablespoon	2 tablespoons
spices:			
pepper	"a pinch"	¹/₄ teaspoon	¹/₂ teaspoon
dill	1 teaspoon	1¹/₂ teaspoons	1 tablespoon±, to taste
fresh parsley, chopped	¹/₂ bunch	1 large bunch	2 large bunches

Cut up chicken and place in large bowl. Add celery, onions, pepper, parsley and dill weed; mix well. Add mayonnaise or salad dressing and lemon juice.

CHILI

	10 PEOPLE	20 PEOPLE	40 PEOPLE
ground beef	2 pounds	4 pounds	8 pounds
onions, chopped	1/2 pound	1 pound	2 pounds
green peppers, chopped	1	2	4
red peppers, chopped	1	2	3
whole tomatoes & juice (Cut up tomatoes into smaller pieces.)	1 28-oz. can	2 28-oz. cans	1 #10 can
tomato sauce	1 29-oz. can	2 29-oz. cans	1 #10 can
kidney beans	2 15^1/2-oz. cans	4 15^1/2-oz. cans	1 #10 can
spices, to taste:			
chili powder	1^1/2–2 tablespoons	3 tablespoons	6 tablespoons
cumin	1 teaspoon	2 teaspoons	1 tablespoon
garlic powder	1 teaspoon	2 teaspoons	1 tablespoon

In large stock pot brown ground beef, onions, red and green peppers and spices with a little water.

When the meat is completely cooked add tomatoes with their juice, tomato sauce and kidney beans. Cook until kidney beans are hot.

Add more spices as needed.

We serve chili with corn chips and choices of extra toppings:

> sour cream
>
> grated cheese
>
> green peppers, chopped
>
> red onions, chopped
>
> tomato, chopped

CORN CHOWDER

	10 PEOPLE	20 PEOPLE	40 PEOPLE
potatoes	1¼ pounds	2½ pounds	5 pounds
onions	½ pound	1 pound	2 pounds
celery	2–3 stalks	½ bunch	1 bunch
creamed corn	2 cup	4–6 cups	1 #10 can
whole corn	2 cups	4–6 cups	1 #10 can
evaporated milk	1 12-ounce can	2 cans	4–6 cans
pepper	to taste	to taste	to taste
salt	to taste	to taste	to taste
bacon	3 slices	6 slices	12 slices
milk	1 quart	½ gallon	1 gallon±
bay leaf	1	2	4

In large stock pot brown bacon which has been cut into small pieces. (You can use oil instead.) Add onions and celery which has been chopped into small pieces and sauté until translucent. Add potatoes and some water. (Do not cover potatoes with water. Water level should be at least 1 inch below potatoes.) When potatoes are slightly tender add corn creamed and whole, evaporated milk, and milk.

If chowder does not seem thick enough remove some potatoes and broth. Mash potatoes and/or thicken with flour. Then add to large pot.

FISH CHOWDER

	10 PEOPLE	20 PEOPLE	40 PEOPLE
potatoes, peeled and chopped	1¼ pounds	2½ pounds	5 pounds
fish (haddock, pollack, or scrod)	3½ pounds	7½ pounds	15 pounds
bacon, sliced in small pieces	3 slices	6 slices	12 slices
onion, chopped	½ pound	1 pound	2 pounds
Atlantic clam juice	1 jar	1 jar	1 jar
Worcestershire sauce (optional)	dash	to taste	to taste
bay leaves	2	3	6
dill	to taste		
basil	to taste		
pepper	to taste		
scallops	⅛ pound	⅛ pound	¼ pound
heavy cream	½ cup	1 cup	2 cups
evaporated milk	½ can	1 can	2 cans
sour cream	½ cup	1 cup	2 cups
milk	1 quart ±	½ gallon	1 gallon ±

NOTE: You can make many substitutions and combinations of dairy. You can use plain milk and less cream or sour cream if you do not want it so rich. I have also made this chowder with non-dairy cream and it was fine.

Peel and chop potatoes into bite-size pieces and place in a separate pot. Cover with water and parboil until almost tender. Drain. Take ¼ of total amount and mash with a little milk. (This will thicken the chowder.)

In a large stock pot cut bacon on the diagonal into small pieces and brown. Add chopped onions and sauté until translucent. Add Atlantic clam juice and spices. If you need more liquid add a small amount of water. Add scallops and let cook for a few minutes. Add fish and cook until fish is white and flaky.

Turn down heat or move to cooler place on stove top or use trivet. Let soup cool a little before adding evaporated milk, heavy cream, sour cream and milk. Add potatoes and mashed potatoes. Bring soup back up to serving temperature.

FRESH FRUIT SALAD

EACH WEEK WE carve a watermelon to make a fresh fruit bowl for lunch. We like to get the passengers involved in carving and designing the "bowl." The mess cook calls for carvers and artists at breakfast to line up interested folks to help out.

We have had some beautiful sculptures made aboard over the years. Whales, loons, sea serpents, and all kinds of boats have sprung out of watermelons. Abstract seascapes have been carved in relief on the sides. The only rule is that we have to be able to serve the fruit salad *in* the watermelon.

FULL BOAT, 40 PEOPLE

> 1 watermelon
> 2–3 green apples
> 2–3 red apples
> 5–6 oranges
> 1 bunch grapes
> 2 cantaloupes
> 1 honeydew melon
> 1 quart strawberries or blueberries when in season
> 4–5 bananas
> 2–3 pears, nectarines or any other fruit available

Wash all the fruit first. Apples, pears and nectarines are cored or pitted and chopped into bite-size pieces. The cantaloupe, honeydew and watermelon can be made into balls or chopped into bite-size pieces. I usually add the bananas at the end, so they don't turn brown and get soft. Ladle fruit into hollowed-out watermelon.

ONION SOUP

	10 PEOPLE	20 PEOPLE	40 PEOPLE
onions, thinly sliced	4¹/₂ 2-pound bags	9 bags	18 bags
butter or margarine	¹/₄ pound	¹/₂ pound	1 pound
spices, to taste:			
cumin	1 teaspoon	2 teaspoons	1 tablespoon
ground pepper	¹/₂ teaspoon	1 teaspoon	1 tablespoon
garlic powder	1 tablespoon	2 tablespoons	3–4 tablespoons
beef, chicken or vegetable base	2–3 teaspoons	1–2 tablespoons	3–4 tablespoons
water	2–3 quarts	1¹/₂ gallons	3 gallons

I know what you're thinking. That's a lot of onions! Onion soup always makes me think of my grandmother, who never skimped on any ingredients. In fact, I think she always added extra; or at least it seemed like it.

Start by putting butter or margarine in the bottom of a large stock pot. Thinly slice the onions and put them on top of the butter or margarine. Add the garlic powder, cumin and ground pepper. Sauté until translucent, on low heat. Then add the water.

Mix the base in a measuring cup and add it to the stock pot once it is all dissolved. Then let the soup come to a boil and continue to boil for 15–20 minutes. Move the pot to a cooler area, or medium heat, taste and add more spices if needed.

We serve our onion soup with grated cheese. If you have a small group you can top off each bowl with a slice of French or Italian bread covered with grated cheese, heated in the oven until the top is golden brown.

QUICHE DU JOUR

ONE PIE, 6–8 SERVINGS

9" pie shell, partially baked	
eggs	3
milk	2 cups
shredded cheddar & Swiss cheese	1½–2 cups
leftovers:	1½–2 cups±
bacon, sausage, lobster, ham,	
spinach salad, tomatoes, broccoli,	
mushrooms, peppers	
salt & pepper	to taste

Mix eggs and milk in medium-size bowl until fluffy and set aside. In the pie shell, layer cheese first, then the meat or vegetable filling, and top off with more cheese. Pour egg and milk mixture over the other ingredients.

Bake at 375° for 45 minutes–1 hour or until a knife inserted off center comes out clean.

TOMATO SOUP

	10 PEOPLE	20 PEOPLE	40 PEOPLE
crushed tomatoes	1 28-ounce can	2 28-ounce cans	1 #10 can
onions	1/2 small	1 small	1 medium
vegetable oil	2 teaspoons	1 tablespoon + 1 teaspoon	3 tablespoons
baking soda	1 teaspoon	2 teaspoons	1 tablespoon
honey	1 tablespoon	2 tablespoons	1/4 cup
evaporated milk	1 can	2 cans	4 cans
half & half or heavy cream	2 cups	1 quart	1/2 gallon
milk	2 cups	1 quart	2 quarts
spices, to taste: dill basil			

Sauté onion sliced in 1/2 circles in vegetable oil. When translucent add crushed tomatoes and move to cooler place on stove or turn down heat. Add spices and let simmer for 20–30 minutes. Add baking soda and honey. (This will make the tomatoes froth). Stir until froth has calmed down. Add evaporated milk, half & half, buttermilk or cream and milk.

VARIATION: If you have leftover lobster it is nice to add lobster pieces to this soup. It makes a great bisque. I add the lobster meat with the crushed tomatoes so it can simmer.

VEGGIE CHILI

	10 PEOPLE	20 PEOPLE	40 PEOPLE
bulgar, raw	3 cups	4–5 cups	6–7 cups
onion, chopped	1½ cups	3 cups	6 cups
green peppers, cut in bite size pieces	2	4	8
red peppers, cut in bite size pieces	2	4	8
carrot, grated	1 cup	2 cups	4 cups
whole tomatoes	1 28-ounce can	2 28-ounce cans	1 #10 can
tomato sauce	1 28-ounce can	2 28-ounce cans	1 #10 can
kidney beans	2 15.5-ounce cans	4 15.5-ounce cans	1 #10 can
spices:			
cumin	1 tablespoon	4–5 tablespoons	6–7 tablespoons
chili powder	1 tablespoon	4–5 tablespoons	6–7 tablespoons
garlic powder	1 teaspoon	1 tablespoon	2 tablespoons
cinnamon	¼ teaspoon	½ teaspoon	1 teaspoon

Heat juice from canned whole tomatoes and pour over raw bulgar. Let stand 15 minutes.

In 3 tablespoons of olive oil, sauté chopped onion, green and red peppers, larger onion pieces and carrots with spices. Cook until tender.

Add whole tomatoes which have been cut into smaller pieces and tomato sauce. Add bulgar and kidney beans.

Cook until bulgar and kidney beans are tender.

VEGGIE STEW

	20 PEOPLE	40 PEOPLE
mushrooms	1 pound	2 pounds
onions	1 pound	2 pounds
tofu	1 block	2 blocks
carrots	1½ bags	3 bags
red potatoes	1 pound	2 pounds
white potatoes	1 pound	2 pounds
broccoli	1 head	2 heads
cauliflower	½ head	1 head
zucchini	3 small	6 small
summer squash	2 small	4 small
tamari	1 cup ±	2 cups ±
spices, to taste:		
cumin		
cayenne pepper		
ginger		
pepper (black)		

In large stock pot put all vegetables and fill halfway with water. Cover and let simmer. Cut tofu into bite size cubes and put in a medium sauce pan with small amount of tamari and small amount of oil. Add the cumin, ginger, mushrooms and onions and sauté in until tender. Add tofu, mushrooms and onions to vegetables, leaving the sauce that is in the medium size sauce pan. Add boiling water (half boat, ½–2 cups; full boat, 3–4 cups) to sauce pan, whisk in flour to thicken. Pour sauce into vegetables. Add more spices and tamari to taste.

Baked Dill Fish

Lori's Baked Fish

Baked Ham

Beef Stew

Lasagna

Lobster Bake

Meat Loaf

Mustard Sauce

New England Boiled Dinner

Roasted Herb Chicken

Scallop Casserole

Turkey

Dinners

Baked Dill Fish

	10 People	20 People	40 People
fish fillets	5 pounds	10 pounds	20 pounds
Pepperidge Farm Herb Stuffing	½ 1-lb. bag	1 1-lb. bag	2 1-lb. bags
celery, chopped	1 stalk	2 stalks	4 stalks
onion, chopped	½ pound	1 pound	2 pounds
sour cream, yogurt, or mayonnaise	¾ pint	1½ pints	3 pints
dill	to taste		
margarine & water	as per package directions		
lemon juice	to taste		

Rinse fresh fish (hake, pollack, or scrod) with cold fresh water. Let drain.

Make stuffing as per directions on bag, but drier. Add chopped onions and celery plus dill weed to water and margarine; bake at 350° until tender. Then add dry stuffing. Mix until moist.

Two variations

1. Spread stuffing into the bottom of baking dish. Place fillets on top of stuffing. Pour lemon juice over each fillet. Then smear sour cream on top of fillets. Sprinkle with dill weed and bake until fish is white and flaky.

2. Spread stuffing onto fillets and roll into rosettes. Place rolled fillets into a large baking dish. Pour lemon juice on fillets. Then spread with sour cream and sprinkle with dill.

LORI'S BAKED FISH

LORI ALEXANDER, WHO cooked on the *Roseway* when Mike and Lynne worked on *Adventure*, cooked baked fish one night for Mike and Lynne; and Mike, who is not a fish guy, liked it well enough to ask Lori for permission to use the recipe on *Angelique*.

	10 PEOPLE 1 PAN 9″x 13″	20 PEOPLE 1 PAN 13″x 18″	40 PEOPLE 2 PANS 13″x 18″
fish fillets	5 pounds	10 pounds	20 pounds
Ritz crackers	1/3 box	3/4 box	1 1/2 boxes
mayonnaise	1 tablespoon	2 tablespoons	1/4 cup
margarine	1/2 stick	1 stick	2 sticks
sea legs, chopped	1/3 package	3/4 package	1 1/2 packages
grated cheese	Sprinkle on top, to taste.		

For fish fillets, I like to use haddock, pollack, or scrod, whichever is best that day.

Rinse and lay fillets in the bottom of a large baking pan, 13″x 18″. In large mixing bowl, crumble up Ritz crackers; add margarine and mayonnaise and mix well. Chop sea legs into small pieces and mix with Ritz crackers. Pour over fish fillets and then sprinkle with grated cheese.

Bake at 350° until it flakes easily with a fork. When I have a full boat it takes 1 1/2 to 2 hours to cook. At home with a smaller amount it will probably take 30–45 minutes to bake. I can't ever remember it taking more than 1 hour.

BAKED HAM

I TALKED TO the butcher and he said that they figure $1/3$ of a pound of meat per person for ham. I use Armour boneless fully cooked ham. It takes two hours for two large hams to get totally heated through. I either put both pieces in one large 13″ x 18″ pan or two 9″ x 13″ pans.

BASTING MIX

FULL BOAT, 40 PEOPLE

Mix together:

brown sugar	3 cups
butter or margarine	1 stick
crushed pineapple	2 8-ounce cans

Score the tops of each ham with diagonal cuts and stud each with whole cloves. Then pour the brown sugar, butter/margarine, pineapple mixture over the top. Put approximately 1–2 cups of water into the bottom of the baking pan. (You want enough water to cover the bottom of the pan, but not more than an inch.) Cover with foil and bake for two hours, basting frequently.

For a smaller piece of meat you would just use a smaller portion of the brown sugar, butter/margarine and pineapple. If you like a more savory flavor, use ground mustard and a tablespoon of apple cider vinegar with the brown sugar. Some folks enjoy maple or honey flavor, so you could use maple syrup or honey instead of the pineapple.

BEEF STEW

	10 PEOPLE	20 PEOPLE	40 PEOPLE
stew beef, cubed	approximately 1/4 pound per person		
onion, chopped	1/2 pound	1 pound	2 pounds
mushrooms	3/4 pound	1 1/2 pounds	3 pounds
potatoes	1 1/4 pounds	2 1/2 pounds	5 pounds
carrots	1 bag	2 bags	4 bags
celery (optional)	1/4 bunch	1/2 bunch	1 bunch
peas, frozen	1/2 bag	1 2-pound bag	2 bags
corn, frozen or canned	1/2 bag	1 2-pound bag	2 bags
			1 #10 can
			6 lbs, 10 ozs
flour	1–1 1/2 cups	1 1/2–2 cups	3–4 cups
garlic powder	1 tablespoon	2 tablespoons	4 tablespoons
pepper	2 teaspoons	1 tablespoon	2 tablespoons
tarragon	2 tablespoons	4 tablespoons	1/4 cup
rosemary	1 tablespoon	2 tablespoons	4 tablespoons
Tabasco sauce	to taste		
Worcestershire sauce	to taste		
Red wine is nice, but optional.	1/2 cup	1 cup	2 cups

Slice onions and mushrooms into large pieces. Place in large stock pot with a small amount of oil or water and Worcestershire sauce. Sauté this mixture on low heat until a natural broth is formed and mushrooms and onions are well cooked.

Peel and wash potatoes and carrots, then cut into bite-size pieces. Set aside. If using celery, wash and cut into small to medium-size pieces.

Mix flour and spices in large mixing bowl. Cut stew beef into smaller pieces if too large and toss into flour-spice mixture. When well covered, brown in cast iron skillet in small amount of oil. Once browned on all sides, place meat into stock pot with onions and mushrooms. Add more water as needed. You need enough to barely cover the meat so it will not stick, but you don't want too much either.

When all the meat has been browned, add the vegetables and just cover with water. Let the mixture simmer on medium heat adding more Worcestershire, Tabasco, spices and red wine to taste. Add the frozen vegetables toward the end since they will not take long to warm up. If you use fresh corn and peas, they will need longer to cook. Keep stirring frequently.

LASAGNA

	20 PEOPLE 1 LARGE PAN, 13″ x 18″	40 PEOPLE 2 LARGE PANS
noodles	1½ boxes	3 boxes
tomato sauce	1½ quarts	1 #10 can
ground beef	3 pounds	6 pounds
onions chopped	1 pound	2 pound
garlic powder		
Italian seasoning	seasonings to taste	
basil		
oregano		
cottage cheese	2½ pounds	5 pounds
ricotta cheese	1–2 pounds	3–4 pounds
grated cheddar & Swiss cheese	1½ pounds	3 pounds ±
eggs	½ dozen	1 dozen

Brown ground beef and onions in a large sauce pan. Add spices and cook until all meat is cooked. Then add tomato sauce. In large mixing bowl mix cottage cheese, ricotta and eggs. Mix well. Place ingredients in layers in large baking pans.

First layer:

> meat sauce to cover bottom of pan
> noodles (Use raw noodles—but make sure that the
>   pan has a lot of liquid in it.)
> cheese mixture & grated cheese
> noodles
> meat sauce

Repeat layers until pan is full, ending with a thick layer of meat sauce.

Cover with foil and bake. On the boat, bake for 2½ hours. At home, bake at 325° for 1½ hours.

SPINACH VARIATION

Tomato sauce: Sauté onions, green pepper, red pepper, and chopped mushroom in 3 tablespoons olive oil.

Add spices: basil, oregano, Italian seasoning and garlic powder, let simmer. Add tomato sauce. Layer as you would meat lasagna.

First layer:

> tomato sauce to cover bottom of pans
>
> noodles
>
> cheese sauce topped with fresh or frozen (drain frozen) spinach and slices of green and red pepper and mushrooms if you prefer. The peppers and mushrooms are optional.
>
> Sprinkle grated cheese on top of spinach.

Repeat layers until pan is full, ending with a large amount of tomato sauce and some grated cheese.

Cover with foil and bake. I bake the spinach lasagna the same as meat.

Zucchini and/or summer squash, sliced the long way, are great if you don't have spinach. And so are sliced tomatoes.

LOBSTER BAKE

IT'S MY NIGHT off! . . . so the assistant and mess cook pack everything we need from the galley for the bake to go ashore by *Angelique's* small boats. Everyone, crew and passengers, pitches in by going out and collecting firewood along the beach. The deck crew then builds the fire on the beach and fills the 10-gallon pot with salt water. Once it starts to boil, the mate throws in the "bugs" (1^1/$_2$–2-lb. lobsters) and corn and covers the whole thing with freshly gathered seaweed. When the lobsters are bright red, they're done. We eat them on the beach and use two rocks to crack 'em open.

> Maine lobsters, 1^1/$_2$–2 lbs., 2 per person & drawn butter
> corn on the cob or baked potatoes
> onion dip
> veggie dip & potato chips
> cheddar & Swiss cheeses with crackers
> carrots & celery sticks and any other veggies you have around
> hot dogs—"For those who know better," says Captain Mike.
> blueberry or strawberry rhubarb pie and
> s'mores

ONION & VEGETABLE DIP

FULL BOAT, **40** PEOPLE

> Onion: 1 box Lipton onion soup mix, dry. I mix 2 packets of soup mix to 2^1/$_2$ pints of sour cream or yogurt. I find that if you mix it several hours before you want to serve it, it tastes better.

> Vegetable: 2 boxes Knorrs dry vegetable soup mix. I mix 2 boxes of soup mix to 2^1/$_2$ pints of sour cream or yogurt. You need to mix it several hours before serving so that the veggies have time to hydrate.

S'MORES

    1 graham cracker
    $1/4-1/2$ chocolate bar
    2 roasted marshmallows

Break graham cracker in half and place chocolate bar on top. Roast 2 marshmallows; when golden brown place on top of chocolate bar and place second half of graham cracker over marshmallows and pull marshmallow off stick. Push the two crackers together.

MEAT LOAF

	20 PEOPLE 3 LOAF PANS	40 PEOPLE 6 LOAF PANS
ground beef	7^1/$_2$ pounds	15 pounds
chopped onions	1 pound	2 pounds
mushrooms	3–4 cups	6–8 cups
bread	^{1}/$_4$ loaf	^{1}/$_2$ loaf
Worcestershire sauce	^{1}/$_4$ bottle	^{1}/$_2$ bottle to taste
ketchup	^{1}/$_4$ cup	^{1}/$_2$ cup
garlic powder	to taste	to taste
pepper	to taste	to taste
eggs	3	6

Mix all ingredients in a large mixing bowl. After mixed well, push into loaf pans (8^1/$_2$" x 4^1/$_4$").

Cover with foil and bake at 350° for 1^1/$_2$ hours. When done, slice in the pans and serve on a platter.

New England Boiled Dinner

I ONCE ASKED the butcher how the brisket was corned. His response was, "Ancient Chinese secret." I have always felt that the success of this meal lies in the great corned beef I get from the market. In addition you need to cook it for at least six hours before you remove it from the stock and cook your vegetables.

	10 PEOPLE	20 PEOPLE	40 PEOPLE
corned beef	5–5$^1/_2$ pounds	10–11 pounds	20–22 pounds
carrots	1$^1/_4$ pounds	2$^1/_2$ pounds	5 pounds
red potatoes	1$^1/_4$ pounds	2$^1/_2$ pounds	5 pounds
white potatoes	$^3/_4$ pound	1$^1/_4$ pounds	2$^1/_2$ pounds
small white onions	$^3/_4$–1 pound	1$^1/_2$–2 pounds	3–4 pounds
cabbages, cut in quarters	2–3 large	3–4 large	6–7 large
spices:			
bayleaves	1–2	3–4	6–8
pepper corns	2 tablespoons	$^1/_4$ cup	$^1/_2$ cup
whole cloves (optional)	1 teaspoon	2 teaspoons	1 tablespoon

Place corned beef in large stock pot and cover with water. Tie spices in cheese cloth and place in pot. Quarter or halve small white onions and put in pot. Cook on medium heat for 4–5 hours. Remove meat, placing in large bowl with some of the broth from pot; cover and set aside.

Put vegetables in broth and cook. About 1 hour before serving place cabbage on top of vegetable to steam. Serve when cabbage is just tender. Reheat meat in oven if necessary.

Serve this meal with broth, vinegar, mustard sauce and horseradish.

I always thought the key to a good New England Boiled Dinner is the meat. I get my corned beef from French & Brawn in Camden. They corn their own beef brisket in a salt and water only brine. You should plan on buying $^1/_2$–$^3/_4$ pounds meat per person.

MUSTARD SAUCE

GREAT WITH NEW England Boiled Dinner.

	10 PEOPLE	20 PEOPLE	40 PEOPLE
In medium mixing bowl combine:			
evaporated milk	¹/₂ can	1 can	2 cans
dry mustard	4 tablespoons ±	9 tablespoons ±	18 tablespoons ±
In medium double boiler heat:			
evaporated milk	¹/₂ can	1 can	2 cans
sugar	¹/₄ cup	¹/₂ cup	³/₄–1 cup

When heated, add contents of medium mixing bowl. Then add 6 egg yolks, one at a time, continuing to stir.

Finally, add some garlic powder and vinegar to taste.

ROASTED HERB CHICKEN

(FUZZY CHICKEN)

	10 PEOPLE	20 PEOPLE	40 PEOPLE
chicken	I use 1 split breast per person and ¹/₂ the total number of people for legs or drumsticks.		
flour	1–2 cups	2–3 cups	4–5 cups
parsley	1 tablespoon	2 tablespoons	4 tablespoons
garlic powder	1 tablespoon	2 tablespoons	4 tablespoons
onion	1 teaspoon	1–2 teaspoons	1 tablespoon
thyme	1 teaspoon	1–2 teaspoons	1 tablespoon
marjoram	1 teaspoon	1–2 teaspoons	1 tablespoon
basil	1 teaspoon	1–2 teaspoons	1 tablespoon
Italian seasoning	2 teaspoons	1¹/₂ tablespoons	3 tablespoons
rosemary	¹/₂ cup	1 cup	2 cups

(Fresh if you have it
 is best, to top it all off.)

Because I make this dish mostly for our Elder Hostelers, I remove most of the skin from the chicken pieces.

Mix the flour and spices in a large bowl, then toss the chicken pieces in the flour and spice mixture until covered with spices.

HOW TO MAKE IT FUZZY:

Place the pieces in a rectangular baking pan and sprinkle more Italian seasoning, parsley, and rosemary (Fresh rosemary is very aromatic.) on the top. This is what makes it fuzzy! Cover with foil.

On the boat it takes 2¹/₂–3 hours to cook 3 pans or 38 chicken breasts and 17 drumsticks at approximately 350°. At home, for a smaller amount, I would think that it would take 1¹/₂–2 hours at 350°–400°. If you remove the foil 15–20 minutes before finished, the top will brown nicely.

SCALLOP CASSEROLE

	8 PEOPLE 1 PAN 9"x 13"	16 PEOPLE 1 PAN 13"x 18"	32 PEOPLE 2 PANS 13"x 18"
scallops (parboiled)	2 pounds	4 pounds	8 pounds
water	1 cup	2 cups	4 cups
cream of mushroom soup, *undiluted*	1$\frac{1}{2}$ cans	3 cans	6 cans
saltines, crushed	8	16	32
American cheese, white	$\frac{1}{2}$ pound	1 pound	2 pounds
baking soda	2 "pinches"	4 "pinches"	8 "pinches"
Worcestershire sauce	1 teaspoon	2 teaspoons	4 teaspoons

Mix all ingredients together and place in greased baking pan. Sprinkle with bread crumbs and bake in medium (350°) oven.

After 10 minutes or so, when bread crumbs start to brown, take a scallop out to test for doneness. Cook just until scallops turn opaque.

TURKEY

I USE A BONELESS turkey breast, two breasts for a full boat, approximately 18–20 lbs. I place the turkey in a large baking dish with about 1 inch of water in the bottom of the pan. Then I sprinkle the top of the meat with ground thyme, marjoram and some melted butter. Cover with foil and bake until cooked through. On board *Angelique* it takes 2 hours to heat through.

STUFFING (made on the stove top)

I use Pepperidge Farm Herb Stuffing and Pepperidge Farm Distinctive Stuffing (Garden Vegetable).

For a full boat, 40 people, I sauté together:

butter or margarine	2 sticks
onions, chopped	2 pounds
celery, chopped	2 cups ±
carrots, chopped (if left from lunch)	1 cup
green apples, chopped	2
red apples, chopped	2
seasonings packet in amount of water from directions	

Let this mixture cook until the vegetables are tender. Add dry mixture, approximately 2½ 1-pound bags for a full boat.

CRANBERRY SAUCE

I use a can of whole berry sauce that is spiced up with zested orange and lemon rind and the juice from both. It's a nice and easy way to make

Three-Bean Salad

Carrot Salad

Cole Slaw

Cucumber Salad

Spinach Salad

Waldorf Salad

Baked Beans

Candied Sweet Potatoes

Green Bean Casserole

Rice Pilaf

Stewed Tomato Casserole

Salads and Veggies

THREE-BEAN SALAD

	10 PEOPLE	20 PEOPLE	40 PEOPLE
green beans yellow (wax) beans red kidney beans chick peas	1 8-ounce can each	1 15^1/$_2$-ounce can each	2 15^1/$_2$-ounce cans each
sweet onion, sliced and separated or chopped	1	2	4
red onion, sliced and separated or chopped	1	2	4
green pepper, cut into strips or chopped	1	2	4

If you prefer to use fresh green and wax beans, you need to blanch them first. Drop them in boiling water as briefly as possible, just until they turn bright green, or yellow for the wax beans.

Marinate in the following dressing 24 hours:

salad oil	^{1}/$_2$ cup	1 cup	2 cups
sugar	^{1}/$_4$ cup	^{1}/$_2$ cup	^{3}/$_4$ cup
cider vinegar	^{1}/$_2$ cup	1 cup	2 cups
pepper	dash, or to taste		
salt	dash, or to taste		
Italian seasoning	1 tablespoon	2 tablespoons	3 tablespoons
basil	1 teaspoon	2 teaspoons	1 tablespoon
oregano	1 teaspoon	2 teaspoons	1 tablespoon

CARROT SALAD
(COPPER PENNIES)

	20 PEOPLE	40 PEOPLE
carrots (sliced in wheels)	2 pounds	4 bags
onion (sliced thin)	1 medium	2 large
salad oil	1/2 cup	1 1/2 cups
vinegar	3/4 cup	2 1/4 cups
green pepper (sliced thin)	2	4
tomato sauce	1 small can	3 small cans
sugar	1/2 cup	1 cup
mustard	1 teaspoon to taste	1 tablespoon
salt & pepper	to taste	

Cook carrots until tender and drain. Add other ingredients and marinate for several hours.

COLE SLAW

	10 PEOPLE	20 PEOPLE	40 PEOPLE
red cabbage	small amount	1/4 head	1/2 head
green cabbage	1/4 head	1/2 head	1 head
vinegar	2 tablespoons	3–4 tablespoons	4–6 tablespoons
sugar or honey	1–2 tablespoons	1/4 cup	1/2 cup
sour cream or yogurt	1/2–3/4 cup	1 1/2 cups	3 cups
salad dressing			
or mayonnaise	1/2–3/4 cup	1 1/2 cups	3 cups

Any or all of these spices can be used, to taste,
to spice up your cole slaw:

cayenne pepper

dry mustard

celery seed

paprika

caraway seeds

garlic powder

Grate or chop cabbage into small pieces. Add remaining ingredients, except spices, to cabbage and mix well.

Add spices to your taste. I like cole slaw sweet and creamy. Some folks like it tangy — use any combination you like.

CUCUMBER SALAD

	6–8 SERVINGS	12–16 SERVINGS	24–32 SERVINGS
cucumbers, sliced paper thin	4	8	16
sour cream or plain yogurt	2 heaping tablespoons	4–5 tablespoons	6–8 tablespoons
sugar	2 tablespoons	2–3 tablespoons	3–4 tablespoons
vinegar	2 tablespoons	3–4 tablespoons	4–6 tablespoons

Mix sour cream, sugar and vinegar. Add to cucumbers.

Place in the refrigerator and let chill. Before serving, mix again to make sure the cucumbers are covered with sour cream mixture.

SPINACH SALAD

ON THE *ANGELIQUE* we always say that spinach salad brings a good breeze to fill the sails and to make it more interesting to eat. Some folks put their corn bread right on top of the salad to hold it down until it's time to eat it.

	10 PEOPLE	20 PEOPLE	40 PEOPLE
spinach (large bags)	1¼	2½	5
cherry tomatoes	¼ pint	1/2 pint	1 pint
mushrooms	½ pound	1 pound	2 pounds
red onions, sliced	1 large	2 large	3 large
hard-boiled eggs (optional)	2	4	8
bacon (optional)	3 strips	6 strips	12 strips

Stem and tear up the spinach first, then give it a good rinse with cold water. Cut the cherry tomatoes into quarters. It's nice to take one or two tomatoes and make a flower shape by cutting around the center in a zigzag fashion, then separating the two pieces.

The mushrooms should be sliced, then rinsed with water. I cut the red onion slices into half circles, usually leaving one in circles to be used as garnish. Save out 2 of the hard-boiled eggs to be sliced into circles for garnish and chop up the rest. Fry the bacon until crispy, then break it into pieces.

Toss together all the ingredients except those that you cut as a garnish. Arrange the garnish.

HOT BOILED DRESSING

If you like a wilted spinach salad, try this dressing.

	10 PEOPLE	20 PEOPLE	40 PEOPLE
water	¾ cup	1½ cups	3 cups
sugar	2 tablespoons±	¼ cup±	½ cup±
vinegar (white or cider)	¾ cup	1½ cups	3 cups
rosemary or dill	1 tablespoons±	2 tablespoons±	3 tablespoons±

Mix water and vinegar in small/medium saucepan on medium heat until warm. Stir in sugar until dissolved. Turn up heat and cook until boiling. Add spice. Let mixture boil for 10–15 minutes, then pour over salad.

WALDORF SALAD

	10 PEOPLE	20 PEOPLE	40 PEOPLE
apples (Cortland or MacIntosh)	1 1/2–2 pounds	3–4 1/2 pounds	6–9 pounds
orange juice concentrate, frozen	3 ounces	6 ounces	12 ounces
vanilla yogurt	1/4 pound	1/2–1 pound	1–2 pound
plain yogurt	1/4 pound	1/2–1 pound	1–2 pound
lemon juice	2 tablespoons	1/4–1/2 cup	1/2–1 cup
raisins (15-ounce box)	1/8 box	1/4–1/2 box	1/2–1 box
walnuts, chopped	1/2 cup	1 cup	2 cups
cinnamon	to taste		
coriander	to taste		

Core and cut apples, with skins on, into bite-size pieces. Put apples into large mixing bowl. Pour lemon juice on apples.

In separate mixing bowl mix thawed orange juice concentrate, yogurts, cinnamon and coriander. When all blended together, pour over apples. Add raisins and walnuts and toss to blend.

BAKED BEANS

WHAT KIND OF beans to start with? That is the question. There are many to choose from; but navy, kidney, Jacob's cattle, soldier, lima and great northern beans seem to be the choices of New Englanders. Lynne McHenry's grandmother would only use soldier beans, and my grandmother used lima or great northern beans. Someone told me that soldier beans are so named because the brown marking on each bean is supposed to be the silhouette of a soldier.

	10 PEOPLE	20 PEOPLE	40 PEOPLE
molasses	1¹/2 cups	3 cups	6 cups
brown sugar	¹/4 pound	¹/2 pound	1 pound
ground mustard	¹/2 teaspoon	1¹/2 teaspoons	1 tablespoon
onions	2 medium	3 medium	6 small
bacon or salt pork	2 strips	4 strips	8 strips
soldier beans	1¹/4 pounds	1¹/2 pounds	5 pounds

My baked beans tend to be sweet. If you prefer a more savory flavor, add more ground mustard. In addition to the above ingredients, my grandmother always added ketsup as well!

I start the beans two days ahead of time on the boat, because I feel beans are best when cooked at a low heat for a long time. They get better with age.

So Sunday night I put the beans in a large stock pot to soak. You want to use plenty of water—there should be several inches of water above the beans. On Monday I parboil the beans. To check if they are done, place some on a spoon and blow on them. If the skins crack they are ready.

In two 4-quart bean pots, peel and cut onions into quarters and divide evenly between two pots. Drain beans and add on top of the onions. Mix the brown sugar, molasses and ground mustard; pour over beans. Cut bacon into small pieces and fry—do not cook completely. Place on top of beans in pot. If the beans are not covered with liquid, add water to cover. Cover the bean pots (I use foil, because the bean pots won't fit into the oven on board with the lids on). I put the bean pots into the oven as soon as I pull dinner out (around 6 PM). I leave the oven on until 8 PM. Then turn it off for the evening, but leave the bean pots in the oven overnight.

In the morning I stir the beans and add more water if they are not covered. I place the bean pots on top of the stove after breakfast and let them come to a boil, at which point I put them on trivets to reduce the heat but still cook. During the afternoon I stir and check to see that they are not getting too dry.

At home I think it would take about 4–5 hours in a 300° oven or at a low temperature all day in a crockpot.

CANDIED SWEET POTATOES

THANKS TO ONE of my first mates, who couldn't stand watching me scorch my fingers peeling hot sweet potatoes, I now peel the potatoes *before* cooking them. In fact, I think it makes them sweeter tasting.

Wash the peeled sweet potatoes, then cut them into medium- to large-size pieces. Place the pieces in bread pans ($8^1/2$ " x $4^1/4$ ").

I usually figure 2 people per large sweet potato.

In a small sauce pan heat:

	10 PEOPLE 2 PANS	20 PEOPLE 3 PANS	40 PEOPLE 6 PANS
water	3 cups	6 cups	12 cups
maple syrup	1 tablespoon	2 tablespoons	$^1/4$ cup
brown sugar	2 tablespoons	$^1/4$ cup	$^1/2$ cup
butter or margarine	$^1/2$ stick	1 stick	2 sticks

Pour the liquid over raw sweet potatoes until they are almost covered, then cover the pan with foil.

Bake in medium oven (350°) until sweet potatoes are tender.

Green Bean Casserole

	10 People 8½" x 4¼" Pan	20 People 9" x 12" Pan	40 People 13" x 18" Pan
cooked green beans	4 cups	8 cups	6 1-lb. bags
cream of mushroom soup	1 small can	2 small cans	1 large can
mushroom pieces	1 small can	1½ cups	3 cups
French-fried onions	1 small can	2 small cans	1 large can

If green beans are frozen: In large sauce pan pour cream of mushroom soup and let soup warm up. Add green beans and mushroom pieces. Let simmer till green beans are warm. If you use canned green beans you do not need to preheat green beans and mushroom soup.

Add ½ of the French-fried onions and pour into casserole dish or rectangular baking pan. Pour the rest of the French-fried onions on top.

Cover with foil and bake ½–1 hour in a medium (350°) oven. Remove foil to brown top.

RICE PILAF

	10 PEOPLE	20 PEOPLE	40 PEOPLE
onions, chopped	1/2 pound	1 pound	2 pounds
mushrooms, chopped			
fresh	1/3 pound	3/4 pound	1 1/2 pounds
or canned	1/2 cup	1 cup	2 cups
white rice (2-pound box)	1/3 box	3/4 box	1 1/2 boxes
butter or margarine	1/4 stick	1/2 stick	1 stick
beef or chicken base	1 teaspoon	2 teaspoons	1 tablespoon

In large sauce pan sauté onions and mushrooms in butter or margarine until tender. Then add rice and let brown for a short time.

Add approximately 11 cups boiling water and 1 heaping tablespoon of beef or chicken base. Cover with foil and lid.

Bring to boil, then place in cooler area of stove top, or reduce heat and place on a trivet until rice is tender.

STEWED TOMATO CASSEROLE

	10 PEOPLE 2 LOAF PANS	20 PEOPLE 3 LOAF PANS	40 PEOPLE 6 LOAF PANS
biscuits	4, or 6 small	8	15
stewed tomatoes	2 small cans	3 small cans	1 #10 can
onions, chopped	$3/4$ cup	$1 1/2$ cups	2 pounds
green pepper, chopped	small amount	$1/2$ pepper	1 pepper
red peppers, chopped	small amount	$1/2$ pepper	1–2 peppers
sugar, to taste	1–2 teaspoons	$1 1/2$ tablespoons	3 tablespoons
flour	2 teaspoons	$1 1/2$ tablespoons	3 tablespoons

spices, to taste:
    pepper
    oregano
    Italian seasoning

Break up biscuits and place a thin layer in the bottom of bread pans. In sauce pan sauté chopped onions and peppers in a small amount of butter or margarine. When tender add stewed and whole tomatoes. Add spices, flour and sugar and let mixture warm up. Pour tomato mixture over biscuits. Break up more biscuits and cover the top of tomato mixture.

Bake in medium oven for 1–$1 1/2$ hours, until top is golden brown. You may need to cover with foil to bake. Remove foil at end to brown top.

Anadama Bread

Banana Bread

Basic Sweet Dough

Breakfast Twists, Braids, and Fans

Steamed Boston Brown Bread

Corn Bread

Cottage Cheese Dill Bread

Garlic Bread

Grapenut Bread

Irish Soda Bread

Sour Cream Coffee Cake

Tri-Colored Bread

Biscuits

Bran Muffins

Doughnut Muffins

Pumpkin Muffins

Breads, Biscuits, Muffins

Anadama Bread

20 PEOPLE, 3 LOAVES

Sprinkle: 1^1/$_4$ cups corn meal into
4^1/$_2$ cups boiling water

Add: 1 cup of molasses
^{1}/$_3$ cup of oil

Cool to lukewarm.

In a separate measuring cup, proof 3 tablespoons
yeast softened in ^{3}/$_4$ cup warm water and 1 teaspoon
molasses. Add to above mixture.

Add: 4^1/$_2$ cups white flour
4^1/$_2$ cups wheat flour

Blend all ingredients in a large bowl until smooth. Add more flour if necessary.

Place in an oiled bowl, butter the top of the dough, cover and let rise until double in bulk. Punch down and shape into three loaves.

Put the loaves into 3 greased loaf pans (8^1/$_2$" x 4^1/$_4$") that have been sprinkled with corn meal. Let loaves rise in pans until twice their original size.

Bake in a 375° oven 30 minutes or until done.

BANANA BREAD

I'VE GOTTEN SEVERAL people hooked on this recipe. I have to send "care pack-ages" sometimes. Most banana bread recipes call for white sugar, but I like to use brown sugar instead. Extra bananas never hurt either.

	15 PEOPLE 1 LOAF	40 PEOPLE 3 LOAVES
brown sugar	1 cup	3 cups
melted butter	2 tablespoons	6 tablespoons
eggs	2	6
ripe bananas	6	14
water	2 teaspoons	3 teaspoons
vanilla	1 teaspoons	3 teaspoons
flour	2 cups	6 cups
baking soda	1 teaspoons	3 teaspoons
chopped nuts (optional)	$^1/_2$ cup	$1^1/_2$ cups

Mix sugar and butter. Add eggs and mix well. Mash bananas in a separate bowl and add water and vanilla. Combine flour and baking soda. Add alter-nately with banana mixture to sugar, butter and eggs. Stir in chopped nuts, if desired.

Bake in greased bread pans ($8^1/_2$" x $4^1/_4$") at 350° for 1 hour or until done.

BASIC SWEET DOUGH
FOR STICKY BUNS AND CRESCENT ROLLS

CAPTAIN MIKE SAYS I like to make them because I like to hear the passengers "ooh" and "ah." I think that they are a sign of my Pennsylvania Dutch heritage. Sticky buns were the first thing I ever made in a Dutch oven!

	10 PEOPLE	20 PEOPLE	40 PEOPLE
milk	1/2 cup	3 cups	6 cups
shortening	1/2 cup	3/4 cup	1 1/2 cups
sugar	1/2 cup	1 cup	1 1/4 cups
eggs	2	3	6
water	1/4 cup (for overnight method)		
yeast	1 tablespoon (If same day use twice as much yeast.)		
honey	1 teaspoon		
flour	4 cups	9 cups	18 cups

BASIC SWEET DOUGH

In a small bowl pour 1/4 cup warm water, 1 tablespoon yeast and 1 teaspoon honey. Set this mixture aside to proof.

In large mixing bowl pour milk, melted shortening, sugar and eggs, mix until well blended. Add the yeast, honey and water mixture once it has proofed. Mix well. Blend in flour until smooth. Place in greased bowl and cover with cloth. Let rise overnight or until doubled in size. Turn out on slightly floured surface and knead.

CRESCENT ROLLS:

Divide kneaded dough into 45 parts. Roll out dough into circles. Spread with butter and, using rotary cutter, cut into pie-shaped wedges. Roll up and pinch into crescent shape. Cover and let rise until twice their size. Bake in medium oven until golden brown.

STICKY BUNS:

Divide kneaded dough into 2 or more parts. Roll out dough on lightly floured surface into a rectangular shape. Spread dough with melted butter, then sprinkle with cinnamon, brown sugar, walnuts and raisins. Roll up dough from long edge and slice into $1^1/_2$-inch segments. Grease a large oblong baking pan and pour a thin layer of maple syrup and/or honey in the bottom. Place segment in the pan so cut edge is down. Cover and let rise until twice their size.

Bake in medium oven until golden brown. You may need to cover the pan with foil if top seems to be cooking too quickly. When done turn over onto foil. Be careful because the syrup from bottom will be very hot and will run down the sides of the buns!

Breakfast Twists, Braids, and Fans

Use sweet dough recipe from sticky buns. You only need one quarter of the total recipe for a twist, braid, or fan recipe.

Fillings & spreads use:

> canned pie fillings: cherry, apple, strawberry rhubarb
>
> jams: raspberry, orange marmalade, apricot, blueberry, strawberry
>
> nuts: walnuts, pecans, almonds, coconut

Some of my favorite combinations:

> orange marmalade & almond
>
> raspberry & coconut
>
> strawberry & almond
>
> apricot & walnut

Prepared Fillings

Lemon & cream cheese

Mix in medium. size bowl, 2 (3-ounce) packages cream cheese, 1 egg yolk, 3 tablespoons sugar, 2 teaspoons lemon juice, 1/2 teaspoon grated lemon peel. Beat until light and fluffy.

Cinnamon & sugar

Granulated sugar with ground cinnamon mixed in, (1 part cinnamon to 3 parts sugar) or to taste. When using this filling you need to spread dough with melted butter first then sprinkle cinnamon-sugar combination on top.

Toppings

Crumb

Mix 1/2 cup white granulated sugar, 1/3 cup white flour, 1/2 teaspoon cinnamon (optional). Blend in 1/4 cup softened butter.

POWDERED SUGAR GLAZE

Mix together in medium sized bowl 1 cup powdered sugar, 2 tablespoons milk, ¹/4 teaspoon vanilla extra extract.

BRAID

Prepare sweet dough. Grease a baking sheet. On a lightly floured board roll out dough to form a 13″ x 8″ rectangle. Place rectangle on greased baking sheet. Spread about ¹/2–1 cup of filling lengthwise on center third of dough. Sprinkle with about ¹/2–³/4 cup nuts or other topping. Along long sides of dough, cut every inch from filling to edge of dough. Fold strips at an angle across filling. Sprinkle crumb topping if desired on top. Cover and let rise in a warm place until double in size. If you are using a crumb topping sprinkle it on the top of dough.

Bake 35 minutes or until golden brown in 375° oven.

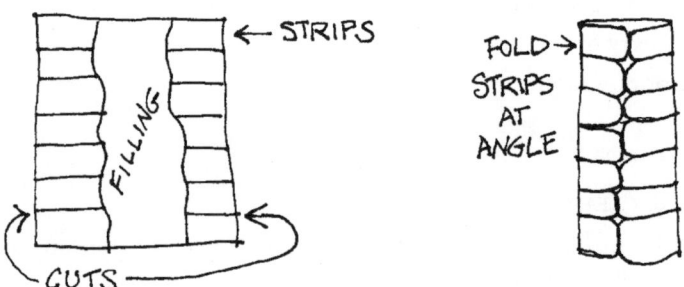

FAN

Prepare sweet dough. On a lightly floured board roll out dough to form a 13″ x 18″ rectangle. Place on greased baking sheet. Spread ¹/2–1 cup of filling over ²/3 of dough and sprinkle with nuts or other topping. Fold the ¹/3 of dough without filling over the center. Fold other side over the other 2 layers, making 3 layers of dough and 2 layers of fill-

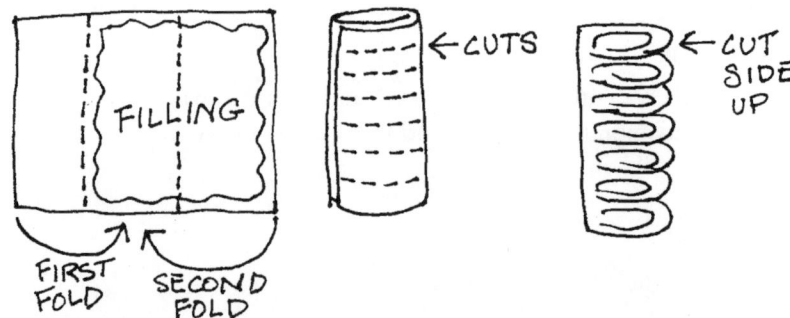

ing. From folded edge cut dough into inch slices ending about 1 inch from opposite side; twist strips so that cut side is up.

Bake in 375° oven for 35 minutes or until golden brown.

TWIST

Prepare sweet dough. Grease a baking sheet. On lightly floured board roll out dough to form a 12" x 9" rectangle. Cut rectangle into 12 3-inch squares. Cut squares diagonal from each corner to about 1/2 inch

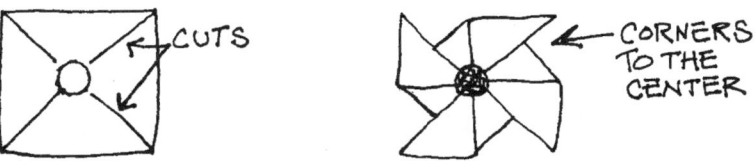

from center. Place squares on greased pan. Spoon 1 tablespoon of filling in center. Bring every other corner to the center of the square, pinch points securely into the center. Cover and let rise in a warm place until double size.

Bake at 400° for 10 minutes or until golden brown.

My favorite filling is lemon & cream cheese.

STEAMED BOSTON BROWN BREAD

THIS RECIPE FILLS three one-pound coffee cans and serves 20 people. To serve 40, simply double the recipe and use 6 coffee cans.

white flour	2 cups
corn meal	2 cups
rolled oats	2 cups
molasses	2 cups
raisins (optional)	1 15.5-ounce box
water	$3^1/_2$ cups
baking soda	2 heaping teaspoons
boiling water	$^1/_2$ cup

Mix dry ingredients in large mixing bowl. Add molasses and the $3^1/_2$ cups water (or 7 cups if you are doubling the recipe). Mix baking soda in the boiling water and add to mixture. Mix well and pour into greased one-pound coffee cans. Cover with foil and place on rack in kettle. Put one inch water in the kettle.

Cover and steam 3 hours. To remove from can, cut bottom and use it to push the loaf out. Let cool a bit before slicing — although this brown bread is dense enough to slice hot.

CORN BREAD

I HAVE TRIED all kinds of variations to this recipe because the deck crew is never satisfied—with a typical recipe for corn bread, crumbs tend to get all over the deck. So the corn bread in this recipe is more moist than most, making it less likely to fall apart.

	10 PEOPLE 8" x 8" PAN	40 PEOPLE TWO 13" x 18" PANS
white flour	1 cup	7 cups
corn meal	1 cup	7 cups
margarine/butter	1/4 cup	1 cup
milk	1 cup	7 cups
eggs	1	7
baking powder	4 teaspoons	7 tablespoons
honey/sugar	1/4 cup	3/4 cup

Combine dry ingredients. Add milk, eggs and melted butter. Mix well and pour into greased pan.

Bake at 425° for 25 minutes or until brown.

For 20 people, it's easy, and best, to halve the 40-people recipe.

VARIATIONS: Add a can of kernel corn and/or grated jalapeño cheese and/or chopped jalapeños.

COTTAGE CHEESE DILL BREAD

TWO LOAVES, 10–15 PEOPLE (For 40 people, I make 6 loaves.)

yeast	1 tablespoon
warm water	1/2 cup
sugar or honey	2 teaspoons
minced onion	2 tablespoons
dill weed	2 tablespoons
	(Fresh is best, but dry is fine.)
creamed cottage cheese	2 cups
baking powder	1 teaspoon
sugar or honey	2 tablespoons
eggs	2
flour	4 1/2 cups

Sprinkle yeast on water, stir until blended, stir in 2 teaspoons sugar or honey. Set aside.

Combine and mix well: cottage cheese, onion, dill, baking powder, 2 tablespoons sugar or honey, and eggs. Add yeast mixture; mix well. Add flour to make stiff dough.

Place in greased bowl; cover. Let rise 1–1 1/2 hours. Punch down; knead. Divide and shape into 2 loaves. Let loaves rise until double their original size.

Bake at 350° for 30 minutes.

GARLIC BREAD

	20 PEOPLE 3 LOAVES	40 PEOPLE 6 LOAVES
yeast	2 tablespoons	3 tablespoons
water	1 cup	2 cups
sugar or/honey	2 teaspoons	1 tablespoon
garlic powder	1 tablespoon	2 tablespoons
water	4 cups	8 cups
white flour	10 cups	20 cups
margarine	$^1/_4$ cup	$^1/_2$ cup

Dissolve yeast in water and honey. Let proof.

In large mixing bowl, add water and garlic powder. Stir in melted margarine. Add yeast. Then mix in flour.

Place in greased bowl, cover with a towel. Set in a warm place and let rise until doubled. Punch down, shape into loaves and place in greased bread pans ($8^1/_2$ " x $4^1/_4$ "). Let rise again.

Bake at 350° until done.

GRAPENUT BREAD

THIS RECIPE I got from Mattie Mosher. She got her nickname, "Mattie," because she's been sailing on windjammers since 1940, when her first cruise was on the schooner *Mattie*. Her favorite seat is still in the bow of the *Mattie* (renamed the *Grace Bailey*).

	20 PEOPLE 2 LOAVES	40 PEOPLE 4 LOAVES
grapenut cereal	1 cup	2 cups
buttermilk	2 cups	4 cups
sugar	1^1/2 cups	3 cups
baking soda	2 teaspoons	4 teaspoons
flour	4 cups	8 cups
butter	4 teaspoons	8 teaspoons
eggs	2	4

Mix grapenuts, buttermilk, sugar, and soda and let stand for 10 minutes. Then add flour, butter and eggs. Mix well.

Bake in greased bread pans (8^1/2" x 4^1/4") at 350° for 1 hour.

IRISH SODA BREAD

ONE LARGE LOAF OR 2 SMALL LOAVES, 10–15 PEOPLE

flour	4 cups
baking powder	1 tablespoon
baking soda	1 teaspoon
sugar	$^1/_4$ cup
coriander	1 teaspoon
butter	$^1/_4$ cup
egg, beaten	1
buttermilk or sour milk	$1^3/_4$ cups

(Optional: Omit coriander and add 2 cups raisins and/or 1 teaspoon caraway seeds.)

Mix dry ingredients: flour, baking powder, baking soda, sugar, coriander. Cut in butter with a pastry cutter or by hand until crumbly. Mix egg with buttermilk. Add milk to dry ingredients and mix until blended.

Turn onto floured board and divide into two loaves or leave as one. Knead slightly and form into round loaf or loaves.

Place in greased pie pan or cookie sheet. Cut a cross into the top of the loaf or loaves.

Bake at 375° for 35–40 minutes until done.

SOUR CREAM COFFEE CAKE

FULL BOAT, 40 PEOPLE, 2 LARGE PANS, 13" x 18"

butter	1^1/$_2$ cups
sugar	3 cups
eggs	9
flour	6 cups
baking powder	3 teaspoons
baking soda	1 tablespoon
sour cream	3 cups

In large size bowl cream butter and sugar. Then add eggs, 3 at a time, and mix until fluffy. In separate bowl mix flour, baking powder and baking soda. Add dry ingredients alternately with butter mixture and sour cream; mix until completely blended. Spread into 2 large greased and floured pans.

TOPPING

brown sugar	1^1/$_2$ cups
flour	2 tablespoons
cinnamon	2 teaspoons
butter	4 tablespoons
pecan	1^1/$_2$ cups

Sprinkle topping on and bake in a medium oven until done—when knife is placed in center and comes out clean.

TRI-COLORED BREAD

EVERYONE WANTS TO know how I get such a nice crust on my bread. It's because of the very hot oven aboard *Angelique*. When I make bread at home it doesn't normally get such a hard crust.

FULL BOAT, 40 PEOPLE, 6 LOAVES

>   3 teaspoons Fleischman's yeast
>   9 cups water
>   3 tablespoons honey
>   6 tablespoons shortening
>   1 cup molasses
>   1/2 cup wheat germ
>   3 tablespoons cocoa
>   3 1/2 cups whole wheat flour
>   3 1/2 cups rye flour
>   13 cups white flour

In 3 separate small bowls mix 1 teaspoon yeast and 1 tablespoon honey with 1 cup warm water; set aside to proof.

WHITE BREAD

In medium size mixing bowl pour 2–3 cups water. Add 2 tablespoons of melted shortening. Add one small bowl of proofed yeast mixture. Then add 6–7 cups white flour, and mix well. Place in greased bowl and cover. Let rise till twice its size.

WHOLE WHEAT BREAD

In medium size mixing bowl pour 2–3 cups water, 1/2 cup molasses, 1/2 cup wheat germ, and 2 tablespoons melted shortening, mix well. Add one small bowl of proofed yeast mixture. Fold in 3 cups white and 3 1/2 cups whole wheat flour; mix well. Place in greased bowl and cover. Let rise until twice its size.

RYE BREAD

In medium size mixing bowl pour 2–3 cups water, 1/2 cup molasses,

3 tablespoons cocoa, and 2 tablespoons melted shortening; mix well. Add last small bowl of proofed yeast mixture. Fold in 3 cups white flour and 3¹/₂ cups of rye flour, mix well. Place in greased bowl and cover. Let rise until twice its size.

When all 3 doughs have risen, one at a time turn out on floured surface and knead. Then cut each loaf into 6 pieces.

Roll out each piece to form a long rope. For each loaf you will need a rope of white, wheat, and rye.

Braid the 3 ropes loosely and place in greased bread pan or on greased cookie sheet. Cover lightly and let rise in a warm place until doubled in size.

Bake at 350° until well browned (approximately 45 minutes to 1 hour).

BISCUITS

THE BISCUITS ARE really good for strawberry shortcake. Just add some extra sugar and vanilla.

	6 PEOPLE	24 PEOPLE	40 PEOPLE
flour	3 cups	12 cups	18 cups
baking powder	2 tablespoons	8 tablespoons	12 tablespoons
margarine	1/4 pound	1 pound	1 1/2 pound
milk	1/2 cup	2 cups	3 cups +
buttermilk	1/2 cup	2 cups	1 quart
sour cream	1/3 cup	1 1/3 cups	1 pint
vanilla	1/8 teaspoon	1 teaspoon	1 tablespoon
sugar	1/8 teaspoon	1 teaspoon	1/4 cup

Mix flour, baking powder and sugar. Blend in margarine. Add wet ingredients and mix thoroughly. Add a little more milk if it is not quite wet enough.

Toss half of dough on a floured board or counter. Toss more flour on top of dough so that you can handle it. Pat down gently until about 1/2 inch thick, cut out biscuits. Place them on a greased cookie sheet.

Bake at 450°–500° for 15–20 minutes until brown and fluffy.

BRAN MUFFINS

YOU CAN DO all kinds of neat things with bran muffins. I usually use the left-over sweet potatoes (just mash them up and add them at the beginning). I've also been known to add left-over apple crisp.

	4 DOZEN	6 DOZEN	8 DOZEN
		FULL BOAT, 40 PEOPLE	
All-Bran cereal	6 cups	9 cups	12 cups
milk	4 cups	6 cups	8 cups
buttermilk	$^3/_4$ ccup	$1^1/_3$ cup	$^1/_3$ cup
eggs	4	6	7
oil	$1^1/_4$ cups	2 cups	$2^1/_3$ cups
flour	$4^1/_3$ cups	$6^1/_3$ cups	$8^3/_4$ cups
baking powder	$2^1/_2$ tablespoons	$3^1/_2$ tablespoons	5 tablespoons
sugar	$^3/_4$ cups±	1 cup±	$1^1/_2$ cups±
cinnamon	2 tablespoons	3 tablespoons	4 tablespoons
raisins, 15.5-ounce box	$^3/_4$ box	1 box	$1^1/_4$ box

NOTE: You can substitute orange juice or apple juice for the milk if it needs to be non-dairy. Also, to decrease cholesterol, use 2 egg whites for each egg and less oil. I once made a small batch with nonfat yogurt instead of oil and used egg white, and they seemed very dense but tasted good.

Measure bran cereal into large mixing bowl. Add milk and butter milk and let soak. Then add eggs, and oil and mix well. Add flour, baking powder, sugar and cinnamon. After all are blended completely and mixed. Finish by adding raisins. Spoon into greased muffin pans or paper liners.

Bake at 350°–375° until brown, 20–30 minutes. (On board *Angelique* it can take as long as 45 minutes to an hour to bake on some days, but usually takes only 30–45 minutes to bake 6 dozen muffins. I can get 4 dozen in the Beaufort oven at one time; and everything has to be rotated left to right, top to bottom and front to back.)

DOUGHNUT MUFFINS

	20 PEOPLE 3 DOZEN	40 PEOPLE 6 DOZEN
vegetable oil	1 cup	2 cups
milk	1^1/$_2$ cups	3 cups
eggs	3	6
flour	4^1/$_2$ cups	9 cups
baking powder	6 teaspoons	4 tablespoons
nutmeg	1^1/$_2$ teaspoons	1 tablespoon
sugar	1^1/$_2$ cups	3 cups

Beat eggs. Add milk and oil; mix together. Sift in flour, baking powder. Add nutmeg and sugar; stir lightly. Spoon into muffin cups; sprinkle top with sugar and cinnamon and dot with butter.

Bake at 400° for 15–20 minutes.

Pumpkin Muffins

	20 People 2 Dozen	40 People 4 Dozen
flour	3 cups	6 cups
sugar	1 cup	1^1/$_2$ cups
baking powder	4 teaspoons	8 teaspoons
cinnamon	^{1}/$_2$ teaspoon	1 teaspoon
nutmeg	^{1}/$_2$ teaspoon	1 teaspoon
milk	1 cup	2 cups
pumpkin	1 cup	2 cups
melted butter	^{1}/$_4$ cup	^{1}/$_2$ cup
eggs	2	4
raisins (optional)	^{2}/$_3$ cup	1^1/$_3$ cups

Mix flour, sugar baking powder, cinnamon nutmeg. Add wet ingredients and mix well.

Bake in greased or lined muffin tin at 375° for 20–25 minutes.

Apple Crisp

Applesauce Spice Cake

Blueberry Buckle

Blueberry Pie

Pie Shell

Blueberry Pudding Cake

Carrot Cake

Chocolate Brownies

Congo Bars

Crazy Chocolate Cake

Derby Pie

Hot Fudge Sauce

Pecan Pie

Pie Crust

Pineapple Upside Down Cake

Raspberry Coconut Squares

Short Cake

Strawberry Rhubarb Pie

Desserts

APPLE CRISP

	10 PEOPLE 1 PAN 9″ x 13″	20 PEOPLE 1 PAN 13″ x 18″	40 PEOPLE 2 PANS 13″ x 18″
cooking apples	1¹/₂ 3-lb. bags	3 3-lb. bags	6 3-lb. bags
lemon juice	1 tablespoon	2 tablespoons	¹/₄ cup
brown sugar	¹/₃ 2-lb. bag	³/₄ 2-lb. bag	1¹/₂ 2-lb. bags
flour	1¹/₂ cups	3 cups	6 cups
cinnamon	to taste, sprinkle on top of apples		
nutmeg	1–2 teaspoons	1–2 tablespoons	3–4 tablespoons
butter or margarine	³/₄ stick	1¹/₂ sticks	3 sticks

Peel, core and slice apples. Pour on lemon juice and toss. Place in the bottom of baking pans. Sprinkle the top of apples with cinnamon.

In separate bowl mix brown sugar, flour and nutmeg. Add butter or margarine and mix until crumbly. Then pour on top of apples and cinnamon.

Bake at 350° until golden brown and apples are soft, which is 45–60 minutes on board, but should only be 30–45 minutes at home.

If the top browns before the apples are done, cover with foil until apples are tender to fork.

Applesauce Spice Cake

15 People, 9″ x 13″ Pan

butter	$^1/_2$ cup
sugar	2 cups
egg	1
applesauce	1$^1/_2$ cups
flour	2 $^1/_2$ cups
cinnamon	$^1/_2$ teaspoon
cloves	$^1/_2$ teaspoon
nutmeg	$^1/_4$ teaspoon
ginger	$^1/_4$ teaspoon
chopped raisins	1 cup
chopped nuts	$^1/_2$ cup
baking soda	2 teaspoons
boiling water	$^1/_2$ cup

Cream butter and sugar. Stir in egg and applesauce. Mix dry ingredients and add alternately with boiling water (in which the soda has been dissolved). Stir in raisins and nuts.

Bake in greased pan at 350° for 30–45 minutes. On board, 45–60 minutes.

Butter cream frosting

butter	1 pound
confectioners' sugar	5 cups
vanilla	dash

In a bowl cream together. Also good with this cake—add rum extract or real rum to flavor the frosting.

BLUEBERRY BUCKLE

	9 PEOPLE 9″ SQUARE PAN	15–20 PEOPLE 9″ X 13″ PAN
brown sugar	3/4 cup	1 1/2 cups
eggs	1	2
flour	2 cups	4 cups
softened butter	1/4 cup	1/2 cup
milk	1/2 cup	1 cup
baking powder	2 teaspoons	3 tablespoons + 1 teaspoon
blueberries	2 cups	4 cups

Cream butter and sugar until smooth. Beat in eggs. Add dry ingredients and mix into large crumbs. Add milk and beat until smooth. Stir in blueberries.

Put into greased and floured pan.

CRUMB TOPPING

brown sugar	1/2–1 cup
flour	1/3–2/3 cup
cinnamon	1/2–1 teaspoon
soft butter	1/4–1/2 cup

Place in bowl and mix until crumbly. Add to top of batter in pan.

Bake at 375° for 45–50 minutes. It takes longer on the boat.

Blueberry Pie

9" PIE, 6–8 PEOPLE

I USE A COMBINATION of fresh and frozen blueberries because the frozen berries give extra juice; fresh berries hold together and keep their shape instead of getting mushy.

fresh blueberries	2 quarts
frozen blueberries	1/2 bag
sugar	1/2 cup ±
lemon juice	1 tablespoon
tapioca	3 tablespoons
cinnamon	small amount

Pour 1/2 bag of frozen blueberries in bottom of pie shell. In large mixing bowl place 2 quarts fresh blueberries, sugar, tapioca and lemon juice and mix well. Pour berry mix on top of frozen berries sprinkle with cinnamon. Cover with second crust or crumb topping.

Bake at 350° for 50 minutes–1 hour until golden brown on top and filling thickens. (It sometimes takes a little longer to bake on the boat.)

PIE CRUST

MY MOM GAVE me this pie crust recipe — it's her favorite — and I've been using it on board *Angelique* ever since.

9" PIE PANS (4–5 CRUSTS)

flour	4–5 cups
lard or shortening	$^3/_4$ pound or $1^3/_4$ cups
sugar	1 tablespoon
egg	1
vinegar	1 tablespoon
cold water	$^1/_2$ cup

I normally use shortening, not lard, aboard the boat. Mix flour and sugar, blend in lard or shortening with pastry blender until mixed. Mix egg and water, then add vinegar and add to flour.

Mix and divide into 4–5 rounds for 4–5 single-crusted pies or 2 double-crusted pies with, possibly, an extra crust left over to use as you like.

Roll the dough out, lay it in the pan, and crimp the edges after filling.

If you don't use the rounds right away, they freeze beautifully. When needed, let thaw and roll out.

BLUEBERRY PUDDING CAKE

	10 People 9" x 13" PAN	20 People 13" x 18" PAN	40 People 2 13" x 18" PANS
blueberries	3 16-ounce bags	4–5 bags	8–10 bags
lemon juice	4 tablespoons	6 tablespoons	10 tablespoons
flour	1¹/₂ cups	3 cups	6 cups
baking powder	1 tablespoon	2 tablespoons	4 tablespoons
nutmeg	1–2 teaspoons	1 tablespoon	2 tablespoons
sugar	¹/₂ cup	1 cup	2 cups
milk	³/₄ cup	1¹/₂ cups	3 cups
eggs	1–2	3	6
melted butter	¹/₃ cup	³/₄ cup	1¹/₂ cups
vanilla	1–2 teaspoons	1 tablespoon	2 tablespoons
sugar	1 cup	2 cups	4 cups
to be sprinkled on top:			
cornstarch	2¹/₂ tablespoons	5 tablespoons	10 tablespoons
boiling water	1 cup	2 cups	4 cups

Place blueberries in the bottom of pan. Sprinkle with the lemon juice. Mix flour, baking powder, nutmeg and sugar. Add milk, eggs and melted butter. Beat until smooth; spread over berries. Mix sugar and cornstarch and sprinkle over dough. Pour boiling water over everything.

Bake at 350° for 45 minutes–1 hour or until top of cake is golden brown and tester comes out dry (cake). The blueberries will get thick like pudding or jelly.

CARROT CAKE

15 PEOPLE, 9″ X 13″ PAN

flour	3 cups
baking powder	2 teaspoons
baking soda	2 teaspoons
eggs	4
oil	1½ cups
sugar	2 cups
grated carrots	2 cups
chopped nuts	1 cup
raisins, floured (optional)	½ cup
cinnamon	2 teaspoons

Place flour, baking powder, baking soda in a large bowl and make a well in the center.

Add: beaten eggs, salad oil and sugar, beat well.

Add: grated carrots, chopped nuts, raisins and cinnamon, and mix well.

Pour into a greased 9″ x 13″ pan and bake at 325° for 1 hour.

CREAM CHEESE FROSTING:

powdered sugar	1 pound
cream cheese	8 ounces
vanilla	1 teaspoon
butter, softened	1 stick
walnuts, chopped (optional)	½ cup

Cream butter and cream cheese. Add sugar, vanilla and mix well. Finish by folding in chopped nuts.

CHOCOLATE BROWNIES

THESE CHOCOLATE BROWNIES have gotten a reputation of their own. I've had various comments from passengers:

> "I picked this boat because of the chocolate brownie recipe. You better be making them."

> "I think these brownies are better than sex."

One passenger talked to her son on the phone during a trip that she came on alone. He said, "Do you think Debbie would send me the left-over brownies and Congo bars?"

They have been referred to as *"you're-going-to-make-those-damn-brownies-again-I-always-eat-too-many."*

	20 PEOPLE ONE 13"x18" PAN	30 PEOPLE ONE 13"x 18" AND ONE 9"x 13" PANS	40 PEOPLE TWO 13"x 18" PANS
unsweet chocolate squares	6	9	12
butter or margarine	¹/₂ pound	³/₄ pound	1 pound
eggs	6	9	1 dozen
sugar	3 cups	4¹/₂ cups	6 cups
vanilla	2 teaspoons	1 tablespoon	1 tablespoon + 1 teaspoon
flour	1³/₄ cups	3 cups	3¹/₂ cups
chocolate chips	1 12-ounce bag	1¹/₂ bags	2 bags
chocolate syrup	¹/₄ cup	¹/₃ cup	¹/₂ cup
walnuts (optional)	2¹/₂ cups	4 cups	5 cups

Melt unsweetened chocolate and margarine or butter. In separate bowl beat sugar and eggs together. Add a few eggs at a time. Add vanilla and mix well. Add melted chocolate and butter or margarine to egg and sugar. Add flour and mix well. Then add chocolate syrup; after blended add chocolate chips and walnuts. Pour into greased pan.

Bake at 325° for 25–30 minutes. Cool the pans on a rack. Cut into squares.

CONGO BARS

15 PEOPLE, 9″ X 13″ PAN

butter or margarine	2/3 cup
brown sugar	1 pound
eggs (a few at a time)	3
vanilla	1 teaspoon
flour	2 1/2 cups
baking powder	2 1/2 teaspoons
chocolate chips	6 ounces
butterscotch chips	6 ounces
chopped nuts (optional)	1 cup

Mix brown sugar and butter until smooth. Then beat in eggs a few at a time. Add vanilla and blend in. Add flour and baking powder and mix well. Add chocolate chips, butterscotch chips and chopped nuts (optional). Pour into greased baking pan.

Bake in a medium oven (350°) 30–40 minutes until golden brown. Cool the pan on a rack. Cut into squares.

CRAZY CHOCOLATE CAKE

WE ONCE HAD chocolate-pudding cake aboard because we tacked so much while it was baking that a layer of pudding formed in the center of the cake.

15 PEOPLE, 9″ X 13″ PAN OR BUNDT PAN

flour	3 cups
sugar	2 cups
cocoa	6 tablespoons
baking soda	2 teaspoons
oil	$^3/_4$ cup
vinegar	2 tablespoons
vanilla	2 teaspoons
warm water,	2 cups
or coffee *or* buttermilk	

Optional coffee or buttermilk — coffee will make it richer and darker; buttermilk will make it lighter.

Mix dry ingredients in a bowl. Add wet ingredients and mix well. Pour into baking pan. If you are using a bundt pan, grease and flour.

Bake in a medium (350°) oven for about 40 minutes, or until tester comes out clean.

This cake is good with regular frosting or a chocolate glaze.

DERBY PIE

I GOT THIS recipe from a friend who told me it is always served at the Kentucky Derby.

9″ PIE, 6–8 PEOPLE

sugar	1 cup
flour	¹/₂ cup
butter, melted	1 stick
eggs, beaten	2
vanilla	1 teaspoon
chocolate chips	1 cup
pecans, chopped	1 cup
pecan halves	1 cup

Combine sugar and flour. Add melted butter, eggs and vanilla. Beat together and then add chocolate chips, chopped pecans and pecan halves. Pour into pie shell.

I always like to cover the top with additional pecan halves. I start on the edge near the crust, placing the pecan halves side by side around the edge and then another row until I get to the center.

Bake 40–50 minutes, until center is firm, in 325° oven.

ICE CREAM

CRANKING ICE CREAM by hand is "a walk down memory lane" for some folks, and others are amazed because they have never made ice cream this way. Folks love to share their favorite memories of cranking ice cream — the stories we've heard!

People have their own special techniques of cranking and mixing the salt and crushed ice. We have two White Mountain ice cream freezers on board. I mix up the ice cream base and my assistant and the mess cook ask for "all hands on deck." They recruit helpers to take turns "sitting on" or "cranking," the ice cream freezers.

To make a batch of ice cream, place the stainless steel canister in the wooden bucket, then layer crushed ice and salt around the canister, attach the crank handle, put a boat cushion on top of the freezer and add one person sitting on top of the boat cushion to keep the freezer from moving around the deck. The cranker then turns the crank handle clockwise at a steady, medium speed. You have to stop from time to time to add more ice and salt. When one person gets tired, another takes over. It should take between 45 minutes and 1 hour to have the finished product. The helpers get to have a pre-taste before dinner.

FULL BOAT (40 PEOPLE), TWO 4-QUART FREEZERS

eggs	2 dozen
granulated sugar	2–3 cups
heavy cream	1/2 gallon (Or use half & half for a lower-fat version.)
all-purpose cream	4–6 pints (Or use 3 quarts 1% milk for low fat.)
vanilla	4 tablespoons

You need to fill the stainless steel canister 3/4 full, so if I need more I add evaporated milk.

We always make one freezer of vanilla and one a different flavor:

MOCHA

instant coffee	3–4 tablespoons
bakers' cocoa (powder)	5–6 tablespoons

MINT OREO COOKIE

peppermint extract	3 tablespoons
Oreo cookies, crushed	¹/₂ bag

The Oreos you add just before the ice cream is hard. You just want to crank enough to mix the cookies through.

CHOCOLATE ALMOND

almond extract	3 tablespoons
powdered cocoa	5–6 tablespoons
almond slivers	3–4 cups

I'm sure you have your own favorite flavor to try.

Hot Fudge Sauce

Full boat, 40 people

In a double boiler melt:

unsweetened chocolate	12 squares (12 ounces)
semi-sweet chocolate chips	1–2 bags (12 ounces)
evaporated milk	3 cans
or heavy cream	2 pints

Stir until melted. Beat until smooth.

Add:

sugar	6 cups
corn syrup	$^3/_4$ cup ± to taste

Blend in:

butter	1 stick
vanilla	2 tablespoons

Beat until smooth.

Serve hot or cold. If too thick add more milk or too thin more chocolate.

PECAN PIE

9″ PIE PAN, 6–8 PEOPLE

white sugar	1 cup
white Karo syrup	1 cup
chopped pecans	1 cup
pecan halves	1 cup
eggs, beaten	2
butter	½ stick

Cream butter and sugar; add beaten eggs, syrup, pecan halves and chopped pecans. Mix well. Pour into pie shell.

Bake at 400° for 15 minutes, reduce heat to 350° and bake 35–45 minutes, or until a silver knife inserted in the center of the filling comes out clean.

PINEAPPLE UPSIDE DOWN CAKE

9" X 13" PAN, 15 PEOPLE

brown sugar	1 cup
butter	1/2 cup
pineapple, sliced or crushed	1 20-ounce can
granulated sugar	1 cup
butter or margarine	2/3 cup
eggs	3
vanilla	2 teaspoons
flour	2 1/2 cups
baking powder	2 1/2 teaspoons
milk	1/2 cup
juice from pineapple	1/2 cup

In rectangular baking pan, mix brown sugar and 1/2 cup butter. Cook and stir over low heat until mixture bubbles. Remove from heat and arrange pineapple slices or cover with crushed pineapple.

In a bowl cream 2/3 cup butter or margarine and the granulated sugar until light. Add eggs one at a time, beating well. Add vanilla. Mix dry ingredients and add to creamed mix alternately with milk and pineapple juice.

Pour batter over fruit and bake at 350° for about 45 minutes.

(Other fruit, like peaches, can be substituted for pineapple.)

RASPBERRY COCONUT SQUARES

		20 PEOPLE ONE 13″ X 18″ PAN	40 PEOPLE TWO PANS
CRUST			
	flour	1½ cups	3 cups
	Graham cracker crumbs	2 cups	4 cups
	sugar	1 cup	2 cups
	margarine	½ cup	1 cup
Add:			
	beaten eggs	2	3–4

Mix with hands to form dough. Press dough into lightly greased pan. Spread raspberry jelly over the crust. (Seedless is nicer but more expensive and harder to find.)

FILLING

Cream:

	softened butter	½ cup	1 cup
	sugar	1 cup	2 cups

Add eggs one at a time; beat until light and creamy:

		2 3 eggs	4–6 eggs

Add:

	coconut	4–5 cups	6–8 cups

Mix well and pour over the crust and jelly. Bake 20–25 minutes at 350° or until golden brown.

SHORT CAKE

FULL BOAT, 40 PEOPLE, 2 LARGE PANS, 13″ x 18″

Bisquick	14 cups
sugar	1 cup
melted butter	1 cup
buttermilk	4^1/$_4$ cups
lemon juice	1 tablespoon
vanilla	2 tablespoons

Mix Bisquick and sugar. Add melted butter, buttermilk, lemon juice and vanilla. Mix well.

Spread into greased pans and bake until golden brown.

If you want less cake just divide the recipe in half.

This is my strawberry shortcake recipe. If you prefer, try the biscuit recipe.

Serve with whipped cream on top.

STRAWBERRY RHUBARB PIE

2 PIES, 12–16 PEOPLE

rhubarb stalks	12
strawberries, fresh	4 pints
strawberries, frozen	1 bag
sugar or honey	1 1/2 cups
tapioca	6 tablespoons

Wash and cut rhubarb into small pieces and place in medium sauce pan. Add 1 bag frozen strawberries and 1/2 cup honey. Cook until rhubarb is tender. Rinse and cut fresh strawberries into halves, place in large mixing bowl. Add 1 cup sugar and 6 tablespoons of tapioca and mix. Add rhubarb mixture when tender to fresh strawberries. Mix well and pour into pie shells.

CRUMB TOPPING

brown sugar	1 1/4 cups
flour	2 1/2 cups
oatmeal	1/2 cup
shortening	1 1/4 cups
cinnamon	to taste

Cover with crumb topping and bake until pie thickens.

This topping is also good on other fruit pies.

INDEX

NOTES

Cover and book design by Russell E. Dockx

Composition by Vicki Fraser

Cover photographs and photographs on pages 27, 35, 49, 67,
83 and 107 by Ted Dillard, ©1997. All rights reserved.

The Angelique Cookbook, Great Recipes from a Windjammer's Galley,
has been set electronically in Galliard CC for text with Mantinia CC
for headlines, both designed by Matthew Carter.

Join us Down East for exciting sailing and exploring, Debbie's fantastic food, Maine islands and sunsets, and relaxation with new friends aboard Angelique!

3, 4, & 6-Day Vacations

ANGELIQUE is your vacation spot in Maine. On *Angelique* you never contend with travel problems — there are no problems finding a place to park, no directions to ask, and no traffic! You get the best of everything a Maine vacation offers: great ocean views, lots of sailing, anchoring every evening in a snug harbor — exploring ashore, Debbie's excellent cooking, and no phones, faxes, e-mail, beepers, no dots, no coms; just pure relaxation.

To make your reservations call or write:

Capt. Mike & Lynne McHenry
PO Box 736
Camden, ME 04843-0736

Call toll free 1 800 282-9989

Visit *Angelique's* web site:
www.midcoast.com/~sailypc

ANGELIQUE

Gaff Topsail Ketch

Length of deck: 95 feet

Beam: 23 feet, $7^1/_2$ inches

Draft: 11 feet

Sail Area: 5269 square feet

Displacement: 142 tons

Passengers: 31

Crew: 7

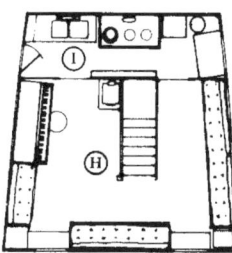

Deck House

Accommodation Plan

A – Crew Quarters

B – Forward Passenger
    Compartment

C – Dining Room

D – Midship Passenger
    Compartment

E – Engine Room

F – Aft Passenger
    Compartment

G – Captain's Cabin

H – Deck House

I – Galley

Cabins:

1 - 2 - 3 - 4 - 5 - 6 - 7 - 8

9 - 10 - 11 - 12 - 14 - 15

One Lower, One upper
Berth

Cabin 16:

One Lower, Two Upper
Berths

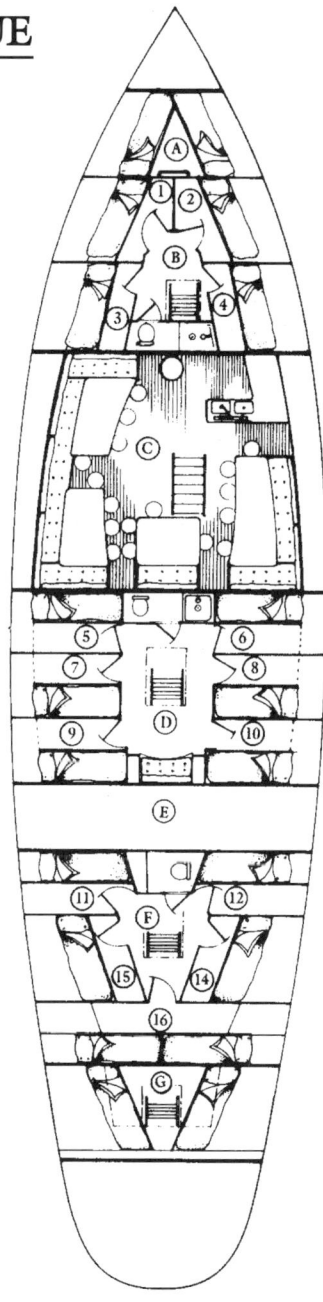